Play-Based Intervention. Spectrum Disorder and Developmental Disabilit

M000279933

Play-Based Interventions for Autism Spe   ʹ   Disorder and Other Developmental Disabilities contains a w   ʹ ʹtion of play therapy interventions for use with children and ʹ ʹ   ʹch autism spectrum disorders, dysregulation issues, or other neurodevelopmental disorders. The structured interventions focus on improvement in social skills, emotional regulation, connection and relationship development, and anxiety reduction. Special considerations for implementing structured interventions and an intervention-tracking sheet are also presented. This valuable tool is a must-have for both professionals and parents working on skill development with these populations.

Robert Jason Grant, Ed.D, LPC, CAS, RPT-S, is a Licensed Professional Counselor, National Board Certified Counselor, Registered Play Therapist Supervisor, and a Certified Autism Specialist. Dr. Grant is a member of the American Counseling Association, Association for Play Therapy, American Mental Health Counselors Association, and the Autism Society of America. He offers training to become a Certified AutPlay Therapy Provider through his website RobertJasonGrant.com and owns a private practice in Missouri where he works with children, adolescents, adults, couples, and families.

Play-Based Interventions for Autism Spectrum Disorder and Other Developmental Disabilities

Robert Jason Grant

Routledge
Taylor & Francis Group

NEW YORK AND LONDON

First published 2017
by Routledge
711 Third Avenue, New York, NY 10017

and by Routledge
2 Park Square, Milton Park, Abingdon, Oxon, OX14 4RN

Routledge is an imprint of the Taylor & Francis Group, an informa business

© 2017 Taylor & Francis

The right of Robert Jason Grant to be identified as author of this work
has been asserted by him in accordance with sections 77 and 78 of the
Copyright, Designs and Patents Act 1988.

Library of Congress Cataloging-in-Publication Data
Names: Grant, Robert Jason, 1971– author.
Title: Play-based interventions for autism spectrum disorder and other
   developmental disabilities / Robert Jason Grant.
Description: New York, NY : Routledge, 2016. | Includes bibliographical
   references and index.
Identifiers: LCCN 2015048764 (print) | LCCN 2016006507 (ebook) |
   ISBN 9781138100978 (hbk : alk. paper) | ISBN 9781138100985
   (pbk : alk. paper) | ISBN 9781315657295 (ebk)
Subjects: LCSH: Play therapy. | Autism in children—Treatment. | Autism
   spectrum disorders in children—Treatment.
Classification: LCC RJ505.P6 G735 2016 (print) | LCC RJ505.P6 (ebook) |
   DDC 618.92/891653—dc23
LC record available at http://lccn.loc.gov/2015048764

ISBN: 978-1-138-10097-8 (hbk)
ISBN: 978-1-138-10098-5 (pbk)
ISBN: 978-1-315-65729-5 (ebk)

Typeset in Sabon
by Apex CoVantage, LLC

Printed and bound in the United States of America by Publishers Graphics,
LLC on sustainably sourced paper.

This book is dedicated to my son, Nolan.

"I am only one, but I am one. I cannot do everything, but I can do something. And I will not let what I cannot do interfere with what I can do."
—Edward Everett Hale

Contents

Foreword

What an honor it is to know Dr. Robert Jason Grant! From our humble beginnings as two therapists traveling the state to attend play therapy workshops, to now conducting workshops of our own, it has been quite a journey. Robert is just one of those people that once you meet you know you have encountered the "real deal." I am privileged to lend some words to Robert's latest book *Play-Based Interventions for Autism Spectrum Disorder and Other Developmental Disabilities.*

As the saying goes, "If you know one person with autism, you know one person with autism." Autism spectrum disorder can be a difficult disability to diagnose and then treat. The emotional toll felt by the child and the child's family can feel overwhelming and exhausting. The amount of community resources can be scarce, and the family may feel pulled in many directions, from the pediatrician and therapist, to the speech/language pathologist and occupational therapist. For this reason, it is vital for all therapists working with autism spectrum disorder to be invested and passionate at finding the best treatment outcome for these children. Dr. Robert Jason Grant has done just that, and his book *Play-Based Interventions for Austin Spectrum Disorder and Other Developmental Disabilities* will be a valued resource for all of us in the field.

Robert's books have been a lifeline to those professionals who work with children on the autism spectrum, as well as other developmental disabilities that cause emotional dysregulation, social skill deficits, and difficulties connecting to others. He offers clear and concise explanations into the primary features of these diagnoses as well as detailed descriptors explaining the symptoms seen in children. The greatest value I have personally gained from Robert's books is the research-based, meaningful interventions to help my clients better regulate emotionally, learn specific social skills, and connect more genuinely with others. I have seen the progress made with each of my clients and know this can be attributed to Robert's theory of AutPlay Therapy and the books he has authored on the subject.

I can say with certainty that any professional reading this book will be pleased and excited to learn additional strategies to use with their clients who have autism or other developmental disabilities. I believe those of us who work with this population have been called to do so, and we are all so very lucky to have Robert on our team.

Tracy Turner-Bumberry, LPC, RPT-S, CAS
Author of *Finding Meaning in Mandalas:*
A Therapist's Guide to Creating
Mandalas with Children

Acknowledgments

There are many great writers, speakers, and advocates for children and adolescents with autism spectrum disorder and special needs. I want to thank each of them for continually inspiring and encouraging me. To all the parents who have participated with me in treatment and entrusted their children to me, I want to give you a special thanks. I have learned more than I can convey from you and your children, and I know your 24-hour-a-day, 7-day-a-week job and the tireless advocacy and effort you put forth to make your child's life better.

Special thanks to Cherie L. Spehar, Audrey Gregan Modikoane, Tracy Turner-Bumberry, Carrie Vaughan Boone, Shannon Anderson, Emma De La Cruz, Tamara Newcomb, Ann Elliot, and John Laskowski for reviewing my book and providing invaluable feedback. You all helped me create a more thorough and thoughtful product. I am greatly appreciative of your time and talents.

Thank you to Liana Lowenstein for all your support, words of wisdom, and generosity and for being a great role model for my efforts. I could not have created what I have without your example.

Thank you to the Association for Play Therapy, the Missouri Association for Play Therapy, and all my play therapy friends and colleagues.

Thank you to Joann Lara: You are a great autism advocate, and you have been a great friend and supporter; I am so happy that our lives connected. You inspired me to move and be active in the change I want to see in the world.

Thanks you to the Amazing Autism Authors, what a great supportive group, that I love being a part of. Thank you to the Southwest Missouri Autism Network (SWAN); Dayna Busch and The Missouri Autism Report; and all of the parents, support groups, and professionals in my community. I learn from you all every day and have felt very blessed to know you all and be a part of our wonderful autism community!

My most important acknowledgment and thanks go to my family and friends for all their support and encouragement and to God for giving me motivation and perseverance when I had none and for gifting me ever so much to write this book. But Jesus looked at them and said, "With man this is impossible, but with God all things are possible" (Matthew 19:26). I am daily grateful and thankful for God and the possible!

Introduction

This book is written for practitioners who work with children and adolescents with autism spectrum disorder (ASD) and other developmental disorders. The terms *autism spectrum disorder*, *ASD*, *developmental disorder*, *developmental disability*, and *neurodevelopmental disorder* may be, at times, used interchangeably where a difference in terminology is not necessary for the information being presented. The play-based interventions listed in this book are designed to improve social skill functioning, emotional regulation, and connection and relationship development. The symptoms listed above often occur at some level in most developmental disorders. The interventions in this book are also designed to address specific learning styles and particulars in skill acquisition that most children and adolescents with developmental disorders possess.

The play-based interventions in this book provide a wonderful treatment approach that meets a child or adolescent at his or her functioning level and assists him or her in gaining needed skills. Practitioners can easily understand and implement the play-based interventions listed in this book and become inspired to create even more play-based interventions of their own. The interventions in this book have been implemented by professionals working in various disciplines, such as mental health therapy, occupation therapy, and speech therapy. Further, interventions have been implemented across various environments including play therapy clinics, schools, residential centers, hospitals, and various clinical and educational settings.

The play-based interventions in this book can be taught to parents, and parents can implement the activities at home with their child and other family members. Special emphasis has been placed on designing interventions in such a way for parents to easily understand and implement the interventions. The more practice a child or adolescent has in working toward improving his or her skill deficits, the better opportunity for achieving gains, and parents can play an important and beneficial role in the process.

This book begins with special considerations in working with children and adolescents with ASD, other developmental disorders. Focus is placed specifically on implementing play-based interventions for these populations, although several practitioners have reported using the interventions in this book for other populations, such as children with ADHD, mood disorders, and adjustment issues. Practitioners should pay special attention to the first section of the book as several points are presented for reflection and consideration before implementing any of the play-based interventions. Fundamentally, this book serves as a tool in implementing a purposeful treatment plan and approach to help children and adolescents gain needed skill development.

1   Treatment Considerations

Autism Spectrum Disorder and Developmental Disabilities

This book is not intended to provide a thorough or in-depth presentation of autism and developmental disorders. The following brief is presented to help practitioners have a better understanding of autism and other developmental disorders as it relates to implementing directive play-based interventions. A suggested reading list is offered in the Appendix for those who desire to increase their knowledge about autism and other developmental disorders.

Autism spectrum disorder (ASD) is a *Diagnostic and Statistical Manual* diagnosis that is usually given after a thorough psychological evaluation where the evaluator measures the child's or adolescent's behavior across a myriad of tests, assessments, and observations. The disorder is considered a spectrum disorder meaning that symptoms vary in intensity from severe to very mild in individuals who have an ASD diagnosis. Common terms used to describe the variance include high or low functioning and severe or mild impairment. Children and adolescents with an ASD will likely have similar problem areas, but the severity of their difficulties and the presence or absence of other features (fine motor clumsiness, normal intelligence, increased or decreased verbal output) will vary (Coplan, 2010).

Children and adolescents with ASD can and usually do exhibit multiple symptoms. The most common symptoms that manifest for each child at some level include impairments in social skills and functioning; impairments in communication; impairments in the ability to self-regulate and modulate emotions; difficulties establishing and creating meaningful relationships and connections with others; restricted, repetitive, and stereotyped patterns of behavior, interests, and activities; sensory processing issues; and difficulties handling transitions and change (Exkorn, 2005).

In regard to play skills, children and adolescents with ASD usually struggle in the areas of pretend or imaginary play and peer or group play. In regard to peer or group play, children and adolescents with ASD typically do desire to have friendships and interact with others peers but simply lack the social ability and skills to interact successfully. Thus, most attempts at some type of interaction usually are met with rejection and anxiety for the child with

ASD. Repeated attempts to engage with peers only to be met with rejection can lead to what others may perceive as a lack of interest in connecting with peers. In reality, this may be a learned behavior to avoid further rejection. Directive play interventions can help children and adolescents learn social skills to interact more successfully with peers and participate more fully in group and peer play.

Pretend and imaginary play skills may also be increased in children with ASD but present a greater challenge. Due to the deficit in pretend and imaginary play, practitioners should avoid play-based interventions that rely heavily on abstract concepts, pretend play, and metaphor (unless specifically working on improving this skill). Play-based interventions should be concrete and clearly communicated to the child and should be literal in addressing the child's issues.

The following example highlights a play approach with a child with ASD. A child with ASD is struggling with a bully at school. In neurotypical play, the practitioner might conduct a puppet show with a frog and fox acting out a bullying scene with the fox bullying the frog and the frog ultimately addressing the issue with an appropriate response and learning some coping skills. For the child with ASD, this may be too much based on metaphor, and the child may not apply the information to his or her situation. A better approach with a child with ASD would be to choose two human puppets and label one the child and the other the child's bully. The practitioner can then act out a bullying scene that actually happened to the child at school and include an appropriate response to the bully. The practitioner can then follow up with the child to make sure he or she understood the story is about him or her and understood the response that he or she could give to the bully. Children and adolescents with ASD are typically concrete and literal thinkers, and they may not apply to themselves or connect with play interventions that rely on metaphor or abstract presentation.

The fifth edition of the *Diagnostic and Statistical Manual* (2013) categorizes ASD as a neurodevelopmental disorder. Other disorders in this category include attention deficit hyperactivity disorder and Tourette's syndrome. There are several other developmental disorders/disabilities that exist as well. The Centers for Disease Control (2014) states that developmental disabilities are a group of conditions due to an impairment in physical, learning, language, or behavior areas. These conditions begin during the developmental period, may impact day-to-day functioning, and usually last throughout a person's lifetime. Common developmental disorders/disabilities include cerebral palsy, fragile X, and Down syndrome. Whether categorized as neurodevelopmental disorders, developmental disorders, or developmental disabilities, these various conditions often share similar symptoms in terms of social function and emotional regulation struggles. Play-based interventions can be helpful in addressing and improving symptom areas associated with these conditions.

Practitioners who work with children and adolescents with ASD or any other developmental disorder should become thoroughly educated about the many aspects related to these complex conditions before implementing play-based interventions or any treatment. Practitioners are encouraged to learn more about ASD and other developmental disorders from diagnosis, to common symptoms, to treatment approaches, to how these conditions affect a child or adolescent and his or her family in a myriad of ways. Proper education about these disorders will enhance and elevate the implementation of play-based interventions for greater success. For editing purposes, this book will often refer to ASD when discussing symptomology that tends to apply to most developmental disorders. The play-based interventions in this book address the commonly shared deficits and struggles that accompany most developmental disorders. These struggle areas include social skills and functioning, emotional regulation, and appropriate relationship connection. Each developmental disorder contains specific and unique characteristics and struggles. Practitioners are encouraged to increase their awareness of the specific developmental disorder that has been diagnosed in the child that he or she is working with.

Relationship Development and Rapport

Regardless of the intervention being used, the practitioner-child relationship is central to the child's realization of treatment goals. The rapport that develops between the practitioner and child forms the foundation for therapeutic success. In building a therapeutic alliance, the practitioner must create an atmosphere of safety in which the child is made to feel accepted, understood, and respected (Lowenstein, 1999). Play-based interventions lend themselves to creating a very structured and directive session with a child or adolescent. The directive element of play-based interventions should not displace the importance for the practitioner and the child to develop good rapport and relationship.

As with any therapeutic approach, it is essential that relationship building be a central focus. Practitioners should spend time in the beginning of treatment and throughout treatment building relationship with children and adolescents, and the parents they are working with. Implementing directive instruction, no matter how great the instruction may be, will be much less effective without proper relationship and rapport between the practitioner and the child. Essentially, it is the relationship that gives the intervention value. Engaging with interventions in the right frame of mind will yield better results.

Treatment Planning and Goal Setting

It is important for practitioners to understand psychological theories and have a theoretical framework from which to work (Cavett, 2010). Directive play-based interventions should always be grounded in a theoretical approach. The interventions in this book align with the AutPlay Therapy protocol for directive play-based interventions to address a child or adolescent with a developmental disorder who is experiencing skill deficits. AutPlay

4 Treatment Considerations

is a treatment approach for children and adolescents with ASD and other developmental disorders. The AutPlay approach is a blending of developmental and behavioral methodology. The foundations of the AutPlay approach include cognitive behavioral therapy, behavioral therapy, and play therapy approaches such as cognitive behavioral play therapy, filial therapy, and Theraplay. Further, AutPlay Therapy incorporates elements from various social skill enhancement programs.

Directive play-based interventions should be specifically chosen to address issues or skill deficits with which an individual child or adolescent is struggling. Interventions should be a component of the child's treatment plan and align with established treatment goals. Practitioners should be able to communicate why interventions are chosen for a specific child, how the intervention will help address the child's identified issues or skill deficits, and how the intervention addresses the child's treatment goals. Practitioners should also implement evaluation procedures to assess that the chosen play-based interventions are actually helping the child improve targeted skill deficits and that the child is making progress toward his or her established treatment goals.

Creating Developmental Disorder Interventions

The play-based interventions listed in this book for ASD and other developmental disorders are purposefully designed to be 1) simple in instruction, 2) low prop based, 3) easily implemented across various environments, and 4) targeted toward specific skill acquisition.

1. **Simple in instruction:** Children with ASD are less likely to focus on, or engage in, an intervention if the instructions are too long or complicated or involve too many steps to complete the intervention. For interventions that may have multiple steps, it is sometimes helpful to present each step one at time and allow the child to complete a step before presenting the next step.
2. **Low prop based:** Children with ASD or other developmental disorders may become distracted or over stimulated with too many toys, props, and expressive art materials around them or available to them. Keeping props simple and focused on the intervention being presented will aid in helping the child maintain focus and engagement and ultimately aid in successful completion of the intervention. Practitioners may even want to present the intervention in an environment that is somewhat sterile and low on possible distractions.
3. **Easily implemented across various environments:** Many different practitioners in various settings work with children with ASD and other developmental disorders. The interventions in this book are designed to be able to transfer across many environments such as a playroom, a school counselor's office, and even an in-home setting where a practitioner or parent may be implementing the interventions.

4. **Targeted toward specific skill acquisition:** The interventions in this book are grounded in a theoretical base and should be chosen for a child or adolescent specifically to address skill deficits or issues that a particular child or adolescent is struggling with. Interventions should align with and be part of the greater treatment plan and goals for the individual child or adolescent involved in therapy.

Practitioners wanting to create their own play-based interventions for children with ASD or other developmental disorders are encouraged to follow the guide listed above and utilize the worksheet located in the Appendix. Some additional points to consider:

- Interventions should be structured, directive, and incorporate a playful approach as much as possible.
- Ideally, interventions should be able to be taught to parents and implemented in the home setting by the parents.
- Consider that interventions may be repeated several times and that the same skill may be addressed with several different interventions.
- Interventions should be adjustable from simple to more complex, should advance in complexity as the child advances, and be applicable to children at different functioning levels.
- Interventions should be concrete and about the child or the child's situation; metaphor and abstract interventions should be avoided.
- Ideally, interventions should incorporate more than one element (social, emotional regulation, anxiety reduction, sensory processing, connection, etc.).
- The practitioner should be flexible in regard to involvement in facilitating the intervention and teaching of new skills; a psychoeducational model is typically implemented.

2 Implementing Directive Play-Based Interventions

The Power of Play

Play is considered the language of all children (Landreth, 1991). The benefits of children engaging in play include cognitive development (learning, thinking, and planning, etc.); social skills (practicing social interaction, roles and routines); language (understanding and talking to others, turn taking, etc.); problem solving (negotiation, asking for help, solving difficulties, etc.); and emotional development (managing feelings, understanding others, empathy, etc.). Children with play skills are more likely to be included with their peers, and play is a key learning tool through which children develop social skills, flexibility, core learning skills, and language. Play also provides opportunities for children to practice events, situations, and routines in a safe place, with no pressure to "get it right" (Phillips and Beavan, 2010).

Sherratt and Peter (2002) suggest that play interventions and experiences are extremely important to children with ASD. They state that simultaneously activating the areas of the brain associated with emotions and generative thought while explicitly teaching children with autism to play will lead to success. Further, Thornton and Cox (2005) conducted individual play sessions with children with ASD specifically to address their challenging behaviors. They incorporated techniques that included relationship development, gaining attention, turn taking, enjoyment, and structure. Their research found that play interventions did impact the child's behavior with a reduction in negative behavior following the structured play interventions.

Cross (2010) stated that no matter what type of play—constructive, outdoor, physical, or cooperative—play helps children learn and developmentally thrive, and the health and productively of a child's play greatly affects later learning. Moor (2008) proposed that play with children with ASD is about structure. In the play context, choice, freedom, and discovery are simply not the things that motivate children with ASD to play in the way they motivate neurotypical peers. Children with ASD need structure because, despite their many differences, in general, they have impaired motivation to interact, learn, and play. They have rigid and repetitive patterns of thinking, and therefore of talking and playing, and are often motivated to preserve sameness.

Many play therapy and play-based treatments can be appropriate interventions in working with children with ASD especially when working with children who have little in the way of social skills and poor communication (Parker and O'Brien, 2011). Play-based interventions are gaining more and more valid research as effective treatment approaches for children and adolescents with ASD and other developmental disorders. Play-based interventions of many types—outdoor, movement, art, music, games, and prop based—provide the opportunity for practitioners to individualize treatment and engage the child in both a playful and structured approach that other ASD treatments may not offer.

This book presents a preferred guide in regard to the play-based interventions listed, indicating what level is appropriate for each intervention. The levels are listed as child, adolescent, or both child and adolescent. Most of the interventions in this book could be used for children ages 3–18 as long as content was adjusted adequately to reflect the child's age. Also, the child's developmental level should be considered as most children with ASD or other developmental disorders will likely present at a younger developmental age than his or her chronological age.

Practitioners should not be hesitant about trying any of the interventions listed in this book with any of the children and adolescents they work with. It will be clear if an intervention is too advanced for the child's chronological or developmental age, and likewise, it will be clear if the intervention is too basic. If a practitioner realizes the intervention is too advanced or too basic, then adjustments can be made to fit the intervention to what is appropriate for that child.

Practitioner Role and Level of Involvement

Children and adolescents with ASD and other developmental disorders will present on a wide continuum in regard to functioning level and ability to understand and complete various directive play-based interventions. The practitioner should be aware of this variance and be prepared to meet each child or adolescent where he or she is in terms of functioning level. The practitioner's involvement in the facilitation, completion, and processing of any intervention will depend on the functioning level of the child. Practitioners should be prepared for their involvement to be anywhere from very directive and involved, providing instruction and stopping to teach appropriate skills, to being an observer and letting the child complete and process an intervention fully on his or her own.

Practitioners should always let the child complete and process through any intervention as much as the child is capable. Thus, if the practitioner is unaware of the child's capability, then he or she should first let the child try before assuming the child is at a functioning level where the practitioner needs to be involved in assisting the child. If a child is having difficulties completing an intervention, the practitioner should become more involved and guide the child through the intervention, breaking it down step by step if necessary.

Practitioners should be prepared to adapt their style and level of involvement at any time even during a session. Children and adolescents with ASD may be able to complete an intervention entirely on their own, may not be able to complete any of the intervention without assistance from the practitioner, or may complete part of an intervention but then become stuck at some point and need assistance from the practitioner. The willingness and flexibility to adjust from observer to educator are key qualities for the practitioner implementing directive play interventions with children with ASD.

Psychoeducational Model

The implementation of directive play-based interventions aligns heavily with a psychoeducational model of treatment. The psychoeducational model is an approach to changing the behavior patterns, values, interpretation of events, and life outlook of children and adolescents who are not adjusting well to their environment(s). Inappropriate behavior is viewed as a child's or adolescent's maladaptive attempt to cope with the demands of that environment. Appropriate behaviors are developed by helping the child or adolescent to recognize the need for change and then helping the child or adolescent to display better behavior choices.

Positive behavioral change is more likely to occur when the practitioner is able to develop and maintain a healthy rapport and relationship with the child or adolescent. This approach involves a combination of both therapeutic approaches and education. According to psychoeducational models, behavioral change comes, not just from the manipulation of environmental variables, but also from the development of a better understanding of self and others and the practice of new ways of reacting. The child or adolescent is taught new ways of responding and the self-control to refrain from using the former inappropriate actions or behaviors (adapted from Tom McIntyre of www.behavioradvisor.com).

Practitioners working with children with ASD and developmental disabilities who are implementing play-based interventions will most likely follow a psychoeducational model. Relationship building and directive instruction are both key elements when working with children with these conditions, and the practitioner should not consider these elements as opposites but as combined features that best serve the child with ASD.

Parental Involvement

Established autism treatments typically involve a parent-training component where parents are taught to implement treatment approaches at home with their child. Play-based interventions are designed to be taught to parents and for parents to implement the interventions at home between sessions. Grant (2012) proposed that parents are the people most knowledgeable about their children and the most equipped with the opportunities to assist their children in everyday situations. Parent training empowers parent to become co-change agents and provides repetition of the intervention; thus, more practice is given to increase skill development.

Booth and Jernberg (2010) stated that a secure attachment relationship is both the outcome of healthy parent-child interaction and the key to long-term mental health. Such a relationship is just as important in helping the child with autism achieve his or her developmental potential as it is with the typically developing child. Further, when parents are part of the treatment, they carry on the successful interactions with the child at home. Home interactions provide the added benefit that the child can generalize from the treatment setting to the home.

Practitioners planning on implementing a parent-training component should establish parent meetings or session times to fully and clearly teach interventions to parents. Practitioners will also want to monitor home implementation carefully to make sure interventions are being implemented at home accurately and successfully. Further, parents will likely have several questions throughout the process, and sufficient time should be allowed to thoroughly address any parent questions or concerns.

A typical structure for a 45–50 minute session may be broken down by meeting with the parents to gain feedback on how things have been going and teaching the parents a new intervention that will be taught to the child and sent home to practice. This may last approximately 15–20 minutes. The remainder of the session will involve meeting with the child and teaching the child the new intervention. This is one example; there are multiple scenarios for meeting with both parents and child. Another option would be to alternate sessions, one week meeting with the parents and the next week meeting with the child. It may also be appropriate to complete the whole session working with both parents and child together, so both are learning the intervention at the same time. The most important element is to make sure there is parent-training time incorporated if interventions are going to be sent home for parents to complete with their child between sessions.

3 Primary Target Areas

Emotional Regulation

When an individual is lacking emotional regulation ability, he or she has difficulty handling emotions and emotional situations. An individual may become overly emotional, may not display emotions, may lack appropriate emotional expression, may not understand or be able to differentiate emotions, may not recognize emotions in others, or may not have any manage or control over his or her own emotions.

Children and adolescents with ASD often struggle with emotional regulation. Managing and modulating both positive and negative emotions can be a challenge, and often without proper ability or training to regulate, these children and adolescents will produce negative, unwanted behaviors when they become dysregulated. Some of the signs of emotional dysregulation include mouthing or chewing on objects or fingers, holding or hording comforting objects, tip-toe walking and rocking back and forth, hand flapping, humming and making random noises, becoming aggressive or noncompliant, becoming withdrawn, removing self from a stressful situation, preoccupation with specific topics/areas of interest, and rigidness in adherence to rules or schedules.

In AutPlay Therapy (Grant, 2016), there are six categories of emotional regulation that children and adolescents with ASD may be lacking: identifying emotions, understanding and expression of emotions, recognizing emotions and situations, recognizing emotions in others, sharing emotional experiences, and managing emotions. Each category can be worked on concurrently or progressively.

The six emotional regulation categories are defined below:

1. **Identifying emotions** refers to a child's ability to identify emotions, accurately label emotions, and reference several emotions as age appropriate.
2. **Understanding and expression of emotions** refers to a child's ability to understand the specific emotions he or she may be experiencing, such as frustration versus anger, and being able to express the emotions that he or she is feeling in an appropriate way, such as verbally communicating his or her feelings to others.

3. **Recognizing emotions and situations** refers to a child's ability to recognize that certain emotions would correspond to certain situations; for example, attending a funeral would make a person feel sad.
4. **Recognizing emotions in others** refers to a child's ability to recognize emotions and emotional expression in other people, such as recognizing when a parent is sad or angry or when another child at school is feeling lonely.
5. **Sharing emotional experiences** refers to a child's ability to mutually participate in sharing emotions with another person, such as connecting with another in excitement while participating in a mutual activity.
6. **Managing emotions** refers to a child's overall ability to manage his or her emotions, such as identifying feelings and being able to express them in an appropriate way and understanding how to handle negative emotions to self-regulate.

Kuypers (2011) proposed that self-regulation is something everyone continually works on, whether they are cognizant of it or not. All people encounter trying circumstances that test their limits from time to time. If children are able to recognize when they are becoming less regulated, they will be able to do something about it to feel better and get themselves to a better place. This comes naturally for some, but for children and adolescents with autism, it is a skill that needs to be taught and practiced.

Play-based interventions that focus on emotional regulation can be individualized to each child and adolescent to work on the regulation issues that a particular child needs to improve. Play-based interventions are natural and playful and, thus, more engaging to children. Many play-based interventions can be implemented several times, both with the practitioner and at home with parents and other family members. Play-based interventions can be implemented until the child or adolescent successfully displays the emotional regulation level or skill that is being sought.

Social Skills and Functioning

The term "social skill" actually functions as an umbrella term, covering a wide range and variety of skills from simple to more complex. Social skills can be anything from learning, to making eye contact, to knowing when a situation is unsafe, to giving a speech in public.

Social skills are interpersonal, specific behaviors that permit an individual to interact successfully with others in an environment. The extent to which an individual is considered to have adequate social skills is determined by others. This is especially true for children and adolescents with an autism disorder or other developmental disability, as they may not be able to fully understand or recognize a social skill even after they have obtained it (Grant, 2012).

Children and adolescents with ASD and other developmental disorders have various levels of impairment in regard to social skills and social functioning. Many fail to develop age-appropriate friendships and have great difficulty understanding the rules of social life. Laushey and Heflin (2000) suggest that impairments in social behavior are so fundamental to children with autism spectrum disorder, that social deficits should be considered the defining feature of autism spectrum disorder.

Dawson, McPartland, and Ozonoff (2002) stated that everyone diagnosed with ASD has trouble with social interchange, specifically with reciprocity, the back-and-forth interaction that make up all social encounters. Further, children and adolescents with ASD tend to have a very limited concept of friendship, tend to face peer rejection, and may struggle in initiating socially encouraging body language. When children and adolescents with ASD are placed in social situations where they do not have the proper social skills to maneuver in the situation, it can create a great deal of anxiety for the child, which typically leads to unwanted behaviors. Just the thought of being put in a situation that is unfamiliar, or where there is a lack of skills to navigate successfully, can also create a great deal of anxiety and lead to unwanted behaviors.

Stillman (2007) suggested the following areas of social interaction and functioning that children and adolescents with autism spectrum disorders tend to have some level of impairment with:

1. Showing and giving affection to caregivers and other important people in the child's life.
2. What appears to be a lack of interest in making friends but actually is a lack of knowing how to engage and make friends.
3. Presenting as very shy or withdrawn.
4. A lack of understanding and recognizing irony, sarcasm, and other forms of humor.
5. A lack of being able to present and show emotions and recognize emotions in others.
6. A tendency to talk too much and about one topic.
7. Randomly talking to him- or herself in public or around others.
8. Performing stimming behavior in social situations such as chewing on his or her shirt or flapping his or her hands.
9. Seeming to be more interested in interacting with others through a computer rather than in person and wanting to spend most of his or her time playing with a computer or video game.
10. Seems to want to, and does better, talking to adults than to children his or her own age.

Dienstmann (2008) proposed that social skills must be taught. The belief that social skills magically appear in children without any development is a common misconception. Research supports social skills training as an evidence-based treatment for learning social skills. It is important to remember that social skills are skills; we all learned them at some point. No matter where a child is at in terms of his or her current social functioning, he or she can learn more social skills.

Connection and Relationship Development

Children with ASD and other developmental disabilities do have a sense of connection and would most likely do poorly if we suddenly took away their caregivers and exchanged them for new ones. That being said, children with ASD and other developmental disabilities do have difficulty showing and expressing connection in meaningful ways and certainly have a difficult time expressing connection in socially typical and acceptable ways (Grant, 2016).

Coplan (2010) stated that children with autism or other developmental disorders have a lack of reciprocity that may be evident from birth, progressing from poor eye contact as an infant or toddler, to difficulty in mastering interactive play as a preschooler, and then to an inability to see things from another person's point of view as a school-aged child.

Lindaman and Booth (2010) described several difficulties that children with ASD have in engagement and connection:

1. Difficulties related to sensory and motor coordination make it challenging to establish rhythm and synchrony with another.
2. Children are less able to imitate and anticipate another person's actions.
3. Difficulty in verbal and nonverbal communication and engaging and shifting attention create challenges in identifying feelings, thoughts, and wants.
4. Children may receive or process information differently.
5. A child's difficulties make it challenging for parents to attune, understand, and respond appropriately, which can lead to more withdrawn behavior by the child.

A lack of connection and of being able to feel a true sense of relationship may be one of the most troubling concerns for parents of a child with an ASD or other developmental disorder. What is happening between child and parent cannot be undervalued. Parents need to feel connection between themselves and their child, and some of that connection needs to be child initiated. Children need to learn connection in healthy and appropriate ways. Ray (2011) proposed that, when children establish closeness with others, they exhibit warmth toward others, seek support from adults with whom they are comfortable, and show enjoyment in their close relationships.

The connection and relationship development interventions in this book are designed to 1) increase connection between the child and caregiver and increase relationship development between the child and other significant relationships; 2) teach children and adolescents how to be more successful in engaging others and increasing relationship connections in an appropriate manner; and 3) provide a fun, natural, play-based atmosphere for children and adolescents to master greater relationship and connection skills.

The connection and relationship development interventions in this book range from simple to more complex by design. Practitioners should pay special attention to the functioning level and age of the child they are working with and choose interventions that match the child's level. Children who have a lower functioning level will likely struggle with the most basic connection-based intervention and may start participating at a minimal level. It is important and appropriate to work with the child's level and progress forward with the child. Forcing a child or adolescent to participate in a connection-based intervention that he or she is uncomfortable with, or that is beyond his or her functioning level, will likely result in the child having a behavior "meltdown" and may result in the child being even more resistant to participating in future connection-based interventions. Many interventions, especially those related to connection and relationship development, involve physical touch. Before implementing interventions that involve physical touch, practitioners are encouraged to review the Association for Play Therapy's "Paper on Touch" that can be found on the APT website at www.a4pt.org.

Children and adolescents with ASD and other developmental disorders seem universally to present a desire for greater connection with others and a longing to have deeper relationship experiences, at least to a level that they feel comfortable with. Consequently, almost universally, children dealing with these issues are not experiencing the level of connection and relationship that they desire and seem to lack the skill level or ability to attain the level of connection they would like to have. Through the consistent and purposeful introduction and practice of play-based interventions designed to increase a child's skill level and ability in making and keeping meaningful connection and relationships, children and adolescents can reach the level of connection and relationship development that they desire. It is likely that each child and adolescent will present with a different goal level in terms of how much connection skill they develop and what level of relationship each child and adolescent is seeking and comfortable with.

It is not necessary for every person, atypical or even neurotypical, to possess the same desire and skill level in relationship development. There is some subjectivity that should be implemented in determining what level of connection ability each child and adolescent may need for general functioning purposes and what level they may want to achieve in terms of greater connection and relationship development.

Additional Services and Support

Many children and adolescents with ASD and other developmental disorders will be involved in multiple treatments. It is common for a child or adolescent to be participating in play therapy treatment as well as occupational therapy, speech therapy, and an applied behavioral analysis (ABA)-based program, and possibly several other types of treatment approaches. Practitioners may also want to refer children and adolescents for additional treatments. It is most helpful when practitioners can correspond with other service providers and establish a comprehensive collaborative treatment approach.

The complexities of ASD and developmental disorders are vast, and mental health professionals and play therapists occupy important roles in the treatment of children and adolescents with ASD and in working with families affected by ASD and developmental disorders. Likewise, other professionals such as occupational therapists, speech therapists, and ABA professionals facilitate important pieces of the treatment puzzle. When all the professionals working with the child can work collaboratively together and with the child's parents, the child is better served.

The play-based interventions in this book have been successfully implemented by mental health practitioners, play therapists, school counselors, occupational therapists, speech therapists, early interventions specialists, and ABA professionals. Any professional reading this book is encouraged to share this resource with other professionals who are working with children and adolescents with ASD and further encouraged to institute a collaborative community referral network in their own community.

Helpful Resources

The Appendix of this book contains helpful resources for the practitioner. There is a feelings list that can be used with interventions that focus on children and adolescents working on emotion identification and expression. Likewise, there is a social skills checklist that can be used to help practitioners identify social skills that children and adolescents need to improve. There is also a toy and material list that can be used to help practitioners identify common toys and materials they will need to complete the directive play interventions described in this book.

The Appendix also includes a play-based intervention-tracking sheet designed to accompany the practitioner's case notes and treatment plan and help the practitioner quickly record and review which directive interventions have been implemented and when the intervention was implemented. A create-your-own-techniques worksheet is provided that gives the practitioner a guide to follow when creating new interventions on their own to implement with clients who have ASD. Several important considerations are presented in the techniques worksheet to guide the practitioner in creating a technique that would be effective with the identified populations that this book addresses.

A list of apps for children and adolescents with ASD and other special needs is presented with a brief description of each. A list of relevant websites and book resources are also listed, which practitioners can access for further reading and knowledge enhancement as well as share with parents.

4 Emotional Regulation Interventions

Emotional Regulation

Confused **Management** Worried

Regulation Silly Control

Affection **Feeling** Expression

Love Closeness Anger

Anxiety *Dysregulated* Sad

Sensory Emotion **Calm**

Excited **Stimulated**

Feelings Pick-Up Sticks

Target Area	Emotional Regulation
Level	Child and Adolescent
Materials	Pick-Up Sticks, Feeling/Color Sheet
Modality	Individual, Family, Group

Introduction

This intervention utilizes the game pick-up sticks to help increase emotional regulation in children and adolescents with ASD. Children and adolescents with ASD and other developmental disorders may need to work on a variety of emotional regulation skills, and this intervention provides the opportunity to individualize the activity to target several different skills that the child or adolescent needs to develop.

Instructions

Using the game pick-up sticks, the practitioner creates a sheet of paper with each pick-up stick color listed and several feelings listed under each color (included here). The practitioner and child play a game of pick-up sticks following the typical pick-up sticks rules. When the child or practitioner picks up a stick of a certain color, he or she must look at the paper and pick one of the feelings listed under that color to share a time that he or she felt that way, act out the feeling, or define the feeling.

Rationale

This technique helps children and adolescents work on identifying, understanding, and expressing emotions. Children also work on fine motor skills and verbal communication with this technique. The practitioner can develop feeling/color sheets that address specific emotions that the practitioner believes the child is struggling in identifying and expressing. It is important to note that some children will have trouble picking up some of the sticks without moving them. The practitioner should be lenient on this rule in the pick-up sticks game, as the point is for the child to acquire a stick so he or she can share a feeling.

Parents can be taught how to play Feelings Pick-Up Sticks, given a feelings sheet, and encouraged to purchase a pick-up sticks game. (They come in various sizes and are usually inexpensive.) The practitioner should encourage parents to implement this intervention regularly a home with their child and, if appropriate, involve the whole family. The game can be played several times, and the feelings sheet can be changed as needed to work on new or more complex emotions. Parents can create their own feelings sheets at home as needed.

Feelings Pick-Up Sticks

RED

Happy • Confused • Scared • Proud

BLUE

Sad • Worried • Loved • Excited

GREEN

Angry • Calm • Nervous • Silly

YELLOW

Brave • Frustrated • Tired • Friendly

BLACK

Peaceful • Anxious

Feelings Beach Ball

Target Area	Emotional Regulation
Level	Child and Adolescent
Materials	Beach Ball, Black Sharpie Pen
Modality	Individual, Family, Group

Introduction

Feelings Beach Ball provides an engaging and fun way for children and adolescents to work on a variety of emotional regulation components. It is also an easy intervention for children and adolescents to take home and play with other family members. The practitioner can complete a beach ball prior to the child attending his or her session and can individualize the ball with specific feelings the child needs to address, or the practitioner and child can work together to create a feelings beach ball.

Instructions

The practitioner blows up a beach ball and instructs the child that they are going to write feeling words all over the ball. (The practitioner could also create a beach ball and write feelings on it prior to the child's session.) The child should think of as many feelings as he or she can, and then the practitioner can add feelings to fill up the beach ball. (The practitioner will want to make sure that feelings are included that the child needs to address.) Once the ball is complete, the practitioner and child toss the ball back and forth. When someone catches the ball, whichever feeling is closest to the person's right thumb is the feeling that he or she has to select and share what makes him or her feel that way or act out the feeling while the other person tries to guess what it is. If someone's thumb lands on a feeling that has already been done, then he or she should choose the next feeling that is closest to his or her thumb. An additional fun element would be to select different ways to toss the beach ball as it is passed back and forth such as "This time, let's hit it to each other with our heads."

Rationale

This technique helps children and adolescents work on identifying, understanding, and expressing emotions and recognizing emotions in others. The child takes the beach ball home, and the practitioner can teach this intervention to the parents to do periodically at home with their child. The child's feelings may change from day to day, and the level that the child is feeling will also change from day to day. Completing this technique periodically at home will help the child learn how feelings can change and how much a person feels a particular feeling can change depending on the situation.

Feelings Beach Ball

List of Feelings

Anxious

Worried

Happy

Sad

Excited

Overwhelmed

Confused

Nervous

Proud

Scared

Frustrated

Loved

Lonely

Rejected

Accepted

Angry

Calm

Friendly

Confident

Peaceful

Tired

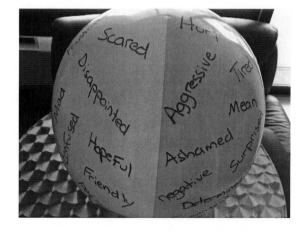

LEGO Emotion House

Target Area	Emotional Regulation
Level	Child and Adolescent
Materials	LEGO Pieces
Modality	Individual, Group

Introduction

Several studies have supported the benefits of using LEGOs with children and adolescents with ASD and other developmental disorders. This intervention uses LEGOs to work on increasing emotional regulation, specifically the identification of emotions. LEGOs are not only naturally inviting for a child but also provide a positive sensory experience and typically are a toy that children with ASD are familiar with.

Instructions

The child is given some LEGOs and instructed to build a house, a building of some type, or a car. The child can also build an abstract object if he or she would prefer. The child is instructed to use different colors, and each color will represent a feeling. The child should choose feelings that he or she experiences often. (The practitioner can also give the child a specific situation or person to identify feelings about such as school or his or her parents.)

Once the child has constructed his or her object, the child goes through the colors and talks about each feeling and what causes him or her to have that feeling. The practitioner may also inquire if the placement of the LEGOs has any significance for the child. The practitioner may also want to create a LEGO Emotion House as well and role model identifying and sharing feelings.

Rationale

LEGO Emotion House helps children and adolescents work on identifying, understanding, and expressing emotions. Children also work on fine motor skills and verbal communication with this technique. The practitioner can teach this technique to parents to do periodically at home with their child. A child's feelings may change from day to day, and the level of emotion that a child is feeling will also change from day to day.

Completing this technique periodically at home will help the child develop better emotional regulation ability. Further, parents can gain a greater understating of what their child is feeling and help their child to express his or her feelings. Practitioners can also use this intervention in a group setting with each child sharing the LEGO Emotion House that he or she has created with the group.

LEGO Emotion House

(Red = Angry, Yellow = Upset, Blue = Sad, Green = Confused, White = Happy)

Construction Feeling Faces

Target Area	Emotional Regulation
Level	Child
Materials	Construction Paper, Glue, Scissors
Modality	Individual, Group

Introduction

This intervention helps children recognize and connect with their emotions. With this intervention, children are able to use expressive materials in a way that allows them to create emotions and discuss the emotions they often experience. Fine motor movements and skills are also involved in the construction of this intervention. Construction Feeling Faces can be completed multiple times, creating several different feeling faces that the child can take home and reference.

Instructions

The practitioner explains to the child that they will be making faces displaying feelings and that the faces will be made completely out of construction paper. The child chooses a piece of paper that he or she cuts into a large circle to represent a head. The child then puts a face on the paper using construction paper only. The child will cut out eyes, eyebrows, ears, nose, mouth, hair, etc. from construction paper. The child is instructed to make a face that displays an emotion. If the child cannot think of any feelings or is unsure how to construct the feeling he or she is thinking of, the practitioner will want to help the child with these processes. The child can cut out any pieces of construction paper and place them in any way that he or she likes on the head, but the overall face must be displaying an emotion. Once the child has completed making the face, he or she shows the face to the practitioner and shares what emotion the face is showing. The practitioner and child discuss the feeling face and when the child has experienced that emotion. The child can make several construction feeling faces and process them with the practitioner.

Rationale

Construction Feeling Faces help children work on identifying emotions and recognizing emotions in others. Children also work on fine motor skills and verbal communication with this technique. The practitioner and child should try to make several Construction Feeling Faces, and all the faces created can be sent home with the child for the child to refer back to and help him or her identify and express feelings at home. The practitioner can teach this technique to the parents to do periodically at home with their child. Parents may want to complete one a day with their child choosing the main feeling that he or she experienced that day.

Construction Feeling Faces

(Happy face)

(Angry face)

Bean Bag Toss

Target Area	Emotional Regulation
Level	Child and Adolescent
Materials	Bean Bags, Bucket
Modality	Individual, Family

Introduction

This is a simple yet engaging intervention that helps children and adolescents work on a variety of emotional regulation skills. The physical movement and challenge piece of Bean Bag Toss are also good for helping children and adolescents learn to better regulate and accomplish a task. With Bean Bag Toss, the practitioner has the ability to individualize the interventions to address the specific emotional regulation needs that the child or adolescent needs to improve upon.

Instructions

Using some type of small bean bag, the practitioner will write a different feeling word on each bean bag. (Square, circle, or animal-shaped bean bags can be purchased through most toy stores—practitioners should purchase a type that can be written on with a Sharpie marker.) The child tries to throw the bean bags into a bucket that is set up somewhere in the room. For each bean bag the child gets in the bucket, the child has to share the definition of the feeling or something that makes him or her feel that way. The practitioner then takes a turn. The practitioner also defines the feeling or shares something that makes him or her feel that way; this provides an educational and role modeling opportunity. The practitioner and child go back and forth trying to get all the bean bags into the bucket and ultimately discussing all the feelings. The intervention can be played several times with new information being shared about each feeling.

Rationale

Bean Bag Toss helps children and adolescents work on identifying, understanding, and expressing emotions. This technique also involves a movement component, and after a couple of rounds, the practitioner should instruct the child that they are now going to play the game using their nondominant hand. Another option is trying to get the bean bags in the bucket by throwing them backwards over the head.

The practitioner should teach this technique to parents to do periodically at home with their child. Other family members may also play this intervention with the child. Multiple people can be involved, creating a fun, social activity that is working on emotional skill development.

Bean Bag Toss

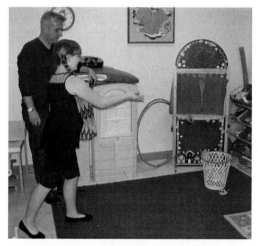

Feelings Spinner Game

Target Area	Emotional Regulation
Level	Child and Adolescent
Materials	Color Spinner, Paper, Pencil
Modality	Individual, Family, Group

Introduction

Children and adolescents with ASD and other developmental disorders often struggle on some level with emotional regulation ability. The Feelings Spinner Game is a simple, low-prop intervention that can be manipulated to work on any emotional regulation skill that a child or adolescent is lacking. Children often enjoy using the spinner format and practitioners can involve children in the planning and setup of the game.

Instructions

Using a color wheel spinner (typically purchased at an education supply store and can be purchased in bulk), the practitioner and child decide what feeling will go with each color on the wheel spinner and write the feelings down on a piece of paper, such as yellow for happy, red for mad, blue for worried, green for sad, etc.

The practitioner and child then take turns spinning the spinner; when someone spins the spinner, whichever color the spinner lands on, the person has to act out the feeling or tell about a time that he or she has felt that way. The same feeling can be landed on several times with new information shared about that feeling. Play continues until the practitioner and child want to stop.

Rationale

The Feelings Spinner Game helps children and adolescents work on identifying, understanding, and expressing emotions. Several different emotional regulation components can be addressed with this intervention. The practitioner can vary the spinner rules by having children, not only make a face displaying or defining a feeling, but even change the rules to make the colors different social skills or coping skills to practice instead of feelings. The spinner should be sent home, and parents should be taught how to play the game and encouraged to play the Feeling Spinner Game several times at home with their child.

Feelings Spinner Game

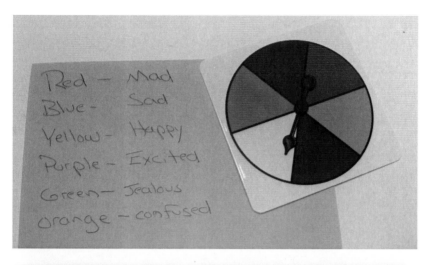

Red — Mad
Blue — Sad
Yellow — Happy
Purple — Excited
Green — Jealous
Orange — confused

Draw My Feelings Face

Target Area	Emotional Regulation
Level	Child and Adolescent
Materials	Paper, Pencil
Modality	Individual, Family, Group

Introduction

Draw My Feelings Face works on several target areas that present struggles for children and adolescents with ASD. This intervention targets improving emotional regulation (identifying and expressing feelings), social skills (understanding body language), and relationship connection (attuning with and noticing another person) in a format that is fun and keeps the child engaged.

Instructions

The practitioner shares with the child that they will practice making and understanding feelings using their faces. The child is given a piece of paper and a pencil. The practitioner makes a feeling face for about 3 seconds. The child has to draw the feeling face the practitioner made and then write on the paper the feeling word that he or she believes goes with the face. The child shows the practitioner, and the practitioner confirms if the child is correct. If the answer is not correct, the practitioner should spend some time talking about what the feeling looks like, what someone would be feeling if they made that face, and practice with the child, possibly using a mirror. The practitioner and child switch roles back and forth with each one making a feeling face and the other drawing and labeling what he or she saw.

Rationale

This technique works on emotional regulation, connection and relationship development, and understanding body language. It is likely that the child will draw some incorrect faces, and when it is the child's turn, he or she will likely make faces that the practitioner cannot understand in terms of what feeling is being shown. These incorrect examples provide opportunity for the practitioner to discuss what a feeling should look like and practice with the child.

Some feelings will be difficult to display with a facial expression, or a facial expression might be appropriate for several different feelings. This provides a good opportunity for discussion on how to handle situations when it is difficult to read a person's body language. This technique also provides a good opportunity for parents and child to work on connection, eye contact, and more accurate emotion expression at home. The intervention can be played repeatedly going through several different emotions.

Draw My Feelings Face

Heart Parts

Target Area	Emotional Regulation
Level	Child and Adolescent
Materials	Foam Piece, Black Sharpie, Various Craft Decorations
Modality	Individual

Introduction

Children and adolescents with ASD commonly struggle with anxiety and worry. High levels of anxiety and worry most often lead to unwanted behavior problems. Multiple sources can create high levels of anxiety in children with ASD, such as a lack of social skills, change, new people or environments, sensory issues, and inability to regulate emotions. This intervention focuses on helping children identify worry and practice ways to self-calm.

Instructions

The child selects a foam piece and cuts the foam piece into 4 different parts. (Practitioners can also have foam pieces available that are already cut into a heart shape.) The 4 parts are labeled: worried, loved, mad, and calm. The practitioner and child begin with the worried part of the heart. The practitioner and child write on the front side of the part all the things they can think of that make the child feel worried. On the back side, the child and practitioner write strategies to help alleviate the negative emotion. The same process is completed for the mad part of the heart.

The child takes the other 2 parts home, and together with his or her parents, writes all the things they can think of that makes the child feel loved and calm on the loved and calm parts of the heart. The child brings the completed parts back to the next session, and the child and practitioner glue the heart together and process through the 4 different feelings, discussing what creates the feelings and helpful coping strategies when experiencing negative feelings. The practitioner and child may want to role-play and practice the identified coping strategies.

Rationale

The Heart Parts intervention works on emotional regulation improvement. The focus is on helping children to identify the feelings they have, what causes those feelings, and coping strategies to address negative feelings. It also helps the child understand that he or she can have different feelings, both positive and negative. The 4 feelings identified can be different from the 4 listed above but should always include worried and calm. Parents are taught to go through the 2 parts that are taken home with their child and further process through identifying and labeling feelings with their child.

Heart Parts

(Front: Four feelings with examples of what creates the feelings)

(Back: Four feelings with strategies to help regulate)

Home and School

Target Area	Emotional Regulation
Level	Child and Adolescent
Materials	Paper, Markers
Modality	Individual

Introduction

Children and adolescents with ASD and other developmental disorders are often in two primary environments, home and school. Often, these two environments hold the most potential for dysregulation and unwanted behaviors. The Home and School intervention is designed to help children identify what emotions he or she is feeling in both settings. Further, it helps children explore what they can do to address the negative emotions in each environment.

Instructions

The practitioner instructs the child to draw a picture of his or her school on one side of a piece of paper and a picture of his or her home on the other side of the paper. The child should write the school's name somewhere on the school picture. The child is then instructed to write all the feelings that he or she has at school somewhere on the school picture and the feelings he or she has at home somewhere on the home picture. The child then shares with the practitioner what makes him or her feel the feelings that he or she has written down.

The practitioner then picks one negative feeling that the child has shared from his or her school and home pictures and asks the child to write on the school and home pictures what he or she thinks that he or she could do at school and home to appropriately express that negative feeling. The practitioner and child then role-play a scenario at school and home where the child appropriately expresses the negative feeling. The practitioner and child can continue until all the negative emotions have been addressed.

Rationale

The focus of this intervention is on helping children and adolescents identify feelings (especially negative feelings) that they are experiencing at school and at home and learn how to express those feelings in appropriate ways. The practitioner and child should try to process through all the negative feelings identified and role-play appropriate expressions for each. Parents can be taught to do this intervention at home and encouraged to role-play through negative feelings daily with their child to help them gain some mastery in both their school and home settings.

Home and School Examples

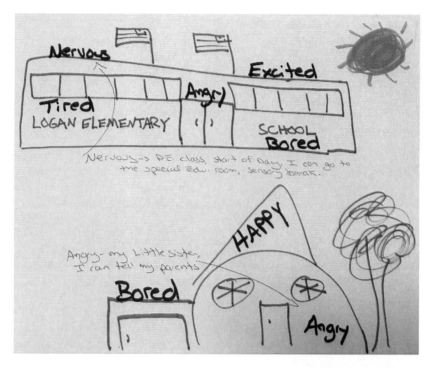

Feelings Don't Break the Ice

Target Area	Emotional Regulation
Level	Child
Materials	Don't Break the Ice Board Game by Hasbro, Stickers
Modality	Individual, Family

Introduction

Don't Break the Ice is a common board game that is naturally engaging for children. This intervention utilizes this popular game to help children differentiate between positive and negative emotions and verbalize what creates certain emotions. The typical game rules are followed with some additional skill development instruction.

Instructions

Using the Don't Break the Ice board game by Hasbro, the practitioner takes each of the "ice" pieces and, on the underside of each piece, puts a color sticker such as a star or heart. There should be 4 different colors represented, and a few of the "ice" pieces should be left blank with no sticker on them. (This is done prior to playing the game with any child.) The practitioner instructs the child that they are going to play Feelings Don't Break the Ice. The practitioner shows the child the stickers on the ice pieces, and the practitioner and child decide together which 2 colors of stickers will represent positive feelings and which 2 colors will represent negative feelings. For example, the practitioner and child might decide that green and blue will be positive feelings and that red and yellow will be negative feelings. The normal Don't Break the Ice rules are observed with an additional rule; once an ice piece is knocked out, if it has a sticker on the underside, the person who knocked that piece out has to identify a positive or negative feeling (depending on the color) and talk about something that has made him or her feel that way. For example, the child knocks out a piece with a yellow sticker on the bottom; the child has to name a negative feeling and then share a time or situation when he or she felt that feeling.

Rationale

This intervention helps children work on increasing emotional regulation ability. The focus is on helping children identify positive and negative feelings and learn how to talk about those feelings. Children with developmental disorders also tend to like the action of hammering the pieces of ice out and putting them back together to play a new game (which also works on fine motor skills). Feelings Don't Break the Ice can be played several times. Parents are encouraged to purchase the game and are taught to do this intervention at home and regularly play with their child. Practitioners should also consider that the colored stickers can be used to represent other skill areas besides feelings, such as social skills, coping skills, or motor movements.

Feelings Don't Break the Ice

Happy Me, Sad Me

Target Area	Emotional Regulation
Level	Child and Adolescent
Materials	Paper, Pencil
Modality	Individual, Group

Introduction

This intervention is simple yet engaging for children and adolescents and presents a strong visual representation of the child's emotions and connecting emotions to situations. Happy and sad are the primary focus, but other feelings can be incorporated such as mad, brave, scared, worried, or calm. Practitioners can choose feelings that the child needs to address and repeat this intervention using different feelings each time.

Instructions

The practitioner instructs the child to draw a line down the middle of a piece of paper. On one side of the paper, the child will draw a happy self and, on the other side, a sad self. Underneath the happy self, the child will write all the things he or she can think of that makes him or her feel happy. Underneath the sad self, the child will write all the things that he or she can think of that make him or her feel sad.

If the child is struggling to identify things that make him or her feel happy and sad, the practitioner can help the child by asking him or her questions, such as "What is your favorite class in school?" "What feelings do you have when you are in that class?" "What is something you don't like to do?" and "What feelings do you have when you have to do that thing?" Once the lists are complete, the practitioner and child go through both lists, talking about each thing the child has identified. At this point, the child could complete another sheet with 2 different emotions.

Rationale

The Happy Me, Sad Me intervention helps children work on increasing emotional regulation ability. The focus is on helping a child identify emotions that he or she is experiencing and having a visual reminder that he or she can reference. Various emotions can be used to complete this intervention, but there should always be a positive emotion that contrasts with a negative emotion. Parents can be taught to complete this intervention at home and encouraged to look for opportunities to play with their child, especially days or times when it may seem their child is experiencing some negative emotions.

Happy Me, Sad Me

Emotion Mane

Target Area	Emotional Regulation
Level	Child
Materials	White Paper Plates, Markers, String, Hole Punch
Modality	Individual, Family, Group

Introduction

Emotion Manes provide children with ASD the opportunity to better recognize the emotions they may be feeling. This is an expressive art intervention that incorporates a visual and tactile component, creating a more sensory experience to aid in acquiring the emotional regulation skills being addressed.

Instructions

The practitioner communicates to the child that they will be creating a mane (like a lion's mane) that the child will be able to wear around his or her face. The practitioner and child cut out the center of a white paper plate. The center piece is thrown away, and the rest of the paper plate ring is colored with different colors. (Only the underside of the plate ring is colored.) Each color represents a different feeling that the child sometimes feels. The feeling word for each color should be written on the inside of the paper plate ring corresponding to the color that represents that feeling. Once the plate has been colored, a hole is punched on each side, and string is used to tie in each hole and make an open mask that can be tied on the child's head. The finished product will resemble a lion's mane. Once the mane is on the child's head, the child should look in a mirror, go through each feeling, and talk about a time or something that has made the child feel that way. The practitioner should discuss with the child how the child has different feelings inside of him or her at different times and how it is OK to feel different emotions and learn to identify them.

Rationale

This technique helps children work on identifying, understanding, and expressing emotions. The child also works on fine motor skills and verbal communication with this technique. Completing this technique periodically will help the child learn how feelings can change from day to day and how much a person feels a certain feeling can change depending on the situation and on different days. If a child is at a more impaired level, then the practitioner may do more of the construction work and assist the child in identifying his or her emotions. Wearing the mane and discussing the feelings while looking in a mirror better helps the child to connect with and take ownership of his or her emotions. These elements also provide a strong visual element to the intervention.

Emotion Mane

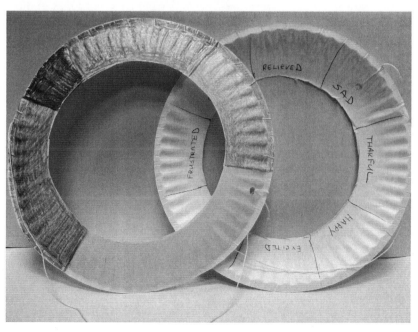

Angry Yes, Calm Yes

Target Area	Emotional Regulation
Level	Adolescent
Materials	White Paper, Construction Paper, Markers, Glue, Scissors
Modality	Individual

Introduction

The Angry Yes, Calm Yes intervention helps adolescents identify situations that make them feel angry or upset and identify calming strategies or interventions to use to help them calm and relax when something is bothering them. Any dysregulating, negative emotion can be addressed besides anger, such as worry, anxiety, frustration, disappointment, or sadness. The practitioner should target the intervention to address specific emotional regulation needs the adolescent is struggling with.

Instructions

The adolescent is instructed to draw an outline of 2 people on a piece of white paper. One person is labeled "angry person," and the other person is labeled "calm person." The practitioner informs the adolescent that both people outlines represent the adolescent. The adolescent picks a colored piece of construction paper for each person outline (one color for the angry person and one color for the calm person). The adolescent cuts out pieces of the colored paper and glues them on each person. On the cut-out pieces of paper for the angry person, the adolescent is instructed to write things that make him or her feel angry and, on the cut-out pieces of paper for the calm person, to write things that make him or her feel calm.

The practitioner may have to help the adolescent identify things that make him or her feel angry and calm. The adolescent then practices the things that make him or her feel calm. The practitioner and adolescent should role-play scenarios using situations or things that the adolescent identified as making him or her angry and then practicing a calming activity.

Rationale

This technique helps adolescents work on identifying, understanding, expressing, and managing emotions. The adolescent should be encouraged to try and apply the calming strategies the next time he or she is feeling angry. The adolescent can take this technique home and practice the calming activities at home. Parents can also be taught how to do this intervention and practice with their child at home.

Angry Yes, Calm Yes Examples

Feelings Card Sort

Target Area	Emotional Regulation
Level	Adolescent
Materials	Several Index Cards, Pen or Pencil
Modality	Individual

Introduction

Adolescents typically have a challenging time communicating their emotions, especially in regard to the relationships in their lives. Feelings Card Sort helps adolescents accurately identify and discriminate between emotions that they may be feeling specifically related to various relationships with family members.

Instructions

The practitioner explains that the adolescent will be using index cards to help identify the various feelings that he or she may have in regard to different relationships in his or her life. The adolescent writes as many feelings as he or she can think of on index cards (one feeling per index card). The practitioner can also add feelings/index cards so there are a variety of feelings represented on the index cards. The adolescent then makes an index card for each family member with the family member's name written on the card. The practitioner takes the family member cards and, one at a time, lays down a family member card. Then, from the feeling index cards, the adolescent chooses the feelings that he or she has for that family member and lays those feeling cards down near the family member card. The practitioner and adolescent then discuss why he or she has those feelings about that family member. The practitioner and adolescent go through this process for each family member card.

An alternate version might be to have the practitioner lay down a family member card and then have adolescent choose feeling index cards that represent the feelings that the adolescent thinks that family member feels. The practitioner and adolescent then discuss why he or she believes that family member would have those feelings. The alternate version is helpful in working on identifying and understating feelings in other people.

Rationale

The Feelings Card Sort intervention helps adolescents work on identifying, understanding, and expressing emotions and identifying emotions in others. The Feelings Card Sort game can be expanded beyond family member relationships and include other people in the adolescent's life such as friends, teachers, doctors, etc.

Feelings Quiz

Target Area	Emotional Regulation
Level	Child and Adolescent
Materials	Paper, Pencil
Modality	Individual

Introduction

The Feelings Quiz helps children and adolescents who are struggling with simply identifying and connecting to feelings. The quiz format provides a fun and engaging way for children to think about feelings and to try and name as many feelings as they can. Practitioners should make the feelings quiz lively, dramatic, and fun.

Instructions

The practitioner instructs the child or adolescent that he or she is going to complete a Feelings Quiz. The practitioner should announce this in a grandiose way and try to keep the process light, not serious like a true formal quiz. The child has to name a certain number of feelings. The number depends on the age and developmental level of the child. The practitioner should try to pick a number that would be challenging yet attainable for the child. It is important that the child be successful in identifying the feelings. The child begins to name off feelings, and the practitioner writes them down to keep track of what has been said and when the target number has been reached.

The practitioner can give hints to help the child identify feelings. An example hint would be to instruct the child to think about a specific place or situation, like school or being on vacation, and what feelings he or she had in that place or situation. Once the child has identified the number required, the practitioner can provide a reward such as a piece of candy or a small prize.

Rationale

This technique helps children and adolescents work on identifying emotions. This technique can usually be done quickly and does not require the whole session, so it can be paired with other techniques. This technique should be done periodically throughout working with the child to see if he or she can progressively identify more feelings. The practitioner can chart the child's increasing ability to identify more feelings without needing any hints. Feelings Quizzes can serve as informal quantitative measures that evaluate the child's ability to increase feeling identification.

Write a Feelings Story

Target Area	Emotional Regulation
Level	Child and Adolescent
Materials	Paper, Pencil
Modality	Individual, Group

Introduction

This intervention helps children more fully conceptualize emotions. The child works on identifying feelings, understanding what may be creating a certain feeling, and recognizing feelings in others. A story format is used so multiple Feelings Stories can be created to present various emotions and situations.

Instructions

The practitioner has the child or adolescent complete a short story that has pre-placed emotion words, for example:

_____ happy _____

_____

_____ sad _____ shy _____

_____ loved _____

_____ angry _____

_____ excited _____ worried _____

_____

The child can write whatever story that he or she wants as long as it includes and makes sense with the pre-placed emotion words that have to be used in the spot they are located in the story. Once the child has completed the story, he or she reads the story to the practitioner. The practitioner can process with the child the story that he or she created. The practitioner may have to assist younger or more impaired children with the writing of the story.

Rationale

This technique helps children and adolescents work on identifying, understanding, and expressing emotions. Fine motor skills and verbal communication are also addressed with this technique. Story templates are included here, but practitioners can easily create their own. Practitioners should let children know that the lines in the template are an approximation as some children may need more room to write out their story between pre-placed feelings. Practitioners can also allow children to create their own templates if desired.

Write a Feelings Story Templates

_____ happy _____

_____

_____ sad _____ shy _____

_____ loved _____

_____ angry _____

_____ excited _____ worried _____

_____

_____ happy _____

_____

_____ sad _____ shy _____

_____ loved _____

_____ angry _____

_____ excited _____ worried _____

_____

_____ happy _____

_____

_____ sad _____ shy _____

_____ loved _____

_____ angry _____

_____ excited _____ worried _____

_____

Feeling Fortune Tellers

Target Area	Emotional Regulation
Level	Child and Adolescent
Materials	Paper, Marker
Modality	Individual, Family, Group

Introduction

Children and adolescents with ASD can struggle with multiple components related to emotional regulation. The Feeling Fortune Tellers intervention provides the opportunity to practice several different areas related to emotional regulation. The practitioner can make the instructions focus on any area of emotional regulation they would like the child to practice, such as sharing about a time you felt that way, showing the feeling on your face, acting out the feeling, telling about a time you noticed someone else feeling this feeling, defining the feeling, or identifying when someone else would feel this emotion. Children typically enjoy the construction and the movement of the fortune tellers and usually want to create multiple fortune tellers.

Instructions

The practitioner explains to the child that they will be creating a paper Feeling Fortune Teller (instructions for completion included here). Fortune tellers should have numbers on the outside, colors on the inside, and feeling words placed on the tab on the other side of the colors. After the fortune teller has been created, the practitioner and child can take turns playing the game.

The basic process of the game is as follows: The practitioner holds the fortune teller in his or her fingers. The child chooses a number, and the practitioner moves the fortune teller back and forth the number of times for the number the child chose. The practitioner opens up the fortune teller, and the child chooses a color. The practitioner lifts the flap for that color, which reveals a feeling. The child has to share something that makes him or her feel that way, act out the feeling, or provide a definition of the feeling.

Rationale

This technique works on emotion identification, expression of emotions, and a variety of emotional regulation struggles. Feeling Fortune Tellers can be made in different sizes and different colors using construction paper. The practitioner and child can play the fortune teller game several times. The child can take their fortune tellers home and play with other family members. Parents can be encouraged to make additional feeling fortune tellers at home with their child. The instructions for creating and playing fortune tellers can be easily accessed online with picture and video examples.

Instructions for Playing the Feeling Fortune Teller Game

The outer layer shows numbers, the practitioner holds the fortune teller, and the child picks a number. The practitioner moves the fortune teller back and forth that many numbers and opens up the fortune teller. The inside shows colors, the child picks a color, and the practitioner pulls up that color and reads the emotion underneath that color. The practitioner and child complete the instruction related to that emotion.

Instructions for Constructing Fortune Tellers

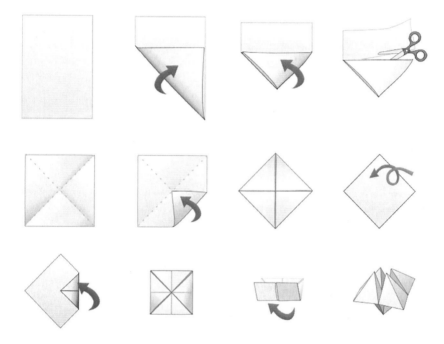

Feelings Puzzle

Target Area	Emotional Regulation
Level	Child and Adolescent
Materials	Blank Puzzle, Markers
Modality	Individual, Family, Group

Introduction

Children and adolescents with ASD and other developmental disorders are often strong visual learners. This intervention provides a strong visual representation of different feelings that children can remember and helps them identify feelings that they may experience regularly. The tactile and puzzle completion component also provides a sense of engagement, order, and creation for the child.

Instructions

The practitioner tells the child they will be using a blank puzzle to create a puzzle focused on feelings. The practitioner instructs the child to write a different feeling word on the back side of each puzzle piece of a blank puzzle. The practitioner may have to help the child think of different feelings and should try to include negative feelings that the child may struggle with. On the front side of the puzzle, the child can decorate the puzzle however he or she wants. Once the puzzle has been completed, the puzzle is taken apart, and the practitioner and child put the puzzle back together. Each time a piece of the puzzle is connected, the child has to share when he or she has felt that feeling or act out what the feeling would look like that is written on each piece of the puzzle.

Rationale

Feelings Puzzles help children and adolescents work on identifying, understanding, and expressing emotions. Children also work on fine motor skills and verbal communication with this technique. The puzzle pieces provide a strong visual representation of feelings for the child, and the action of taking apart and putting the puzzle back together helps strengthen the child's familiarity with the targeted emotions. Children should take their puzzles home and put them together with their parents and work with their parents on sharing and identifying feelings. Parents and children can also make new puzzles with different feeling words. Blank puzzles come in several sizes and various numbers of pieces. A good basic size for children is a small puzzle with 9 pieces. Puzzles with more pieces might be selected for adolescents. A good website for purchasing blank puzzles is www.blank-puzzles.com.

Feelings Puzzle

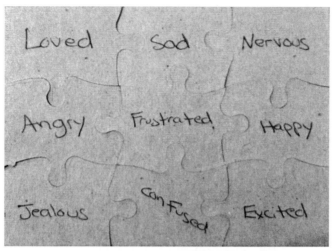

(Back of puzzle: Each piece has a feeling written on it)

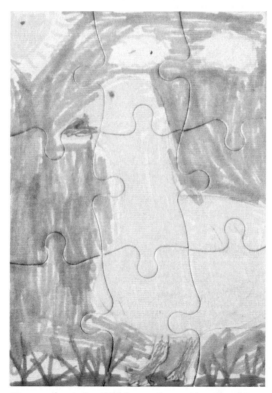

(Front of puzzle: Child can draw whatever he or she wants)

Paint Swatch Degrees of Feelings

Target Area	Emotional Regulation
Level	Child and Adolescent
Materials	Paint Swatches, Pen
Modality	Individual, Group

Introduction

Children and adolescents with ASD often struggle with differentiating among feelings. Basic feelings such as happy, sad, and mad may be identified, but more specific variances of each may be challenging. This intervention helps children identify and better understand a more wide range of emotional expression.

Instructions

Using a paint swatch that has several shades of color (see example included here), the child is instructed to write down all the forms of certain feelings that he or she can think of. Common feeling categories include anger, sadness, happiness, and anxiety. For example, the practitioner might label one paint swatch "angry"; the child would then have to think of feelings that are similar to angry. The child might write "irritated," "enraged," "annoyed," and "frustrated." Typically, the child will create a paint swatch for happy, sad, and mad. Once the child has written all the forms of these feelings that he or she can think of, the practitioner can add to it if there are some that the child has missed.

Once the feelings have been written down, the child is instructed to rank them from the one he or she feels most often to the one he or she feels least often. Once the ranking is complete, the practitioner and child process through the highest-ranked feelings and discuss what makes the child feel that way.

Rationale

Paint Swatch Degrees of Feelings helps children and adolescents work on identifying, understanding, and expressing emotions and understanding degrees of feelings. The practitioner should use the different shades of color to emphasize to the child the different feelings that may have similar components. For example, lonely and rejected may feel similar to sad. This intervention is helpful to increase a child's awareness of the various nuances in emotions. New paint swatches can be made for different feelings, and a general feeling swatch can be made displaying the main feelings identified by the child. Paint swatches can be acquired for free at various hardware and paint stores. Paint swatches should be sent home with the child for the child to reference and continue to work on accurately identifying what he or she is feeling.

Paint Swatch Degrees of Feelings Examples

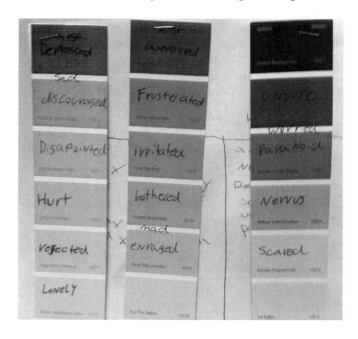

Paper Feeling Balloons

Target Area	Emotional Regulation
Level	Child and Adolescent
Materials	Paper, Markers, Pencil, Balloons
Modality	Individual

Introduction

Paper Feeling Balloons is a fun and engaging way to help children think about different situations and the feelings that they may experience in each situation. Children are often able to identify more feelings by thinking of specific situations, environments, or people and recognizing feelings they have in regard to specific qualifiers.

Instructions

The child is instructed to draw 1 large balloon on a piece of paper. The child is instructed to write as many feelings as he or she can think of inside the large balloon. This is the master balloon the child will be referring back to. The child is then instructed to draw 4 smaller balloons on the paper; each balloon should be a different color. The practitioner takes the paper and labels one of the smaller balloons a subject, such as "school." In that balloon, the child then writes all the feelings that he or she can think of that he or she feels about school. The child can reference his or her master balloon. If he or she thinks of a feeling that was not written in the master balloon, then he or she writes that feeling in both the school balloon and the master balloon. When the child is finished with the school balloon, he or she gets a real balloon that he or she can keep and take home. This is repeated for the other 3 balloons with the practitioner labeling each one a different subject and the child identifying feelings that he or she has in regard to that subject.

Some subject ideas might include school, home, mom, dad, siblings, music class, Boy Scouts, the doctor's office, playing video games, etc. The practitioner should try to pick subjects that will produce a wide variety of feelings for the child. When all the balloons have been completed, the practitioner and child can discuss all the feelings that the child identified.

Rationale

This technique helps children and adolescents work on identifying, understanding, and expressing emotions. It also helps children understand that they can have more than one feeling about a subject and that some of those feelings might be a mix of both positive and negative feelings. Children are typically able to identify more feelings by having them consider specific situations and the feelings they have in that situation. Children can take this intervention home and complete more feelings balloons with their parents.

Paper Feeling Balloons Examples

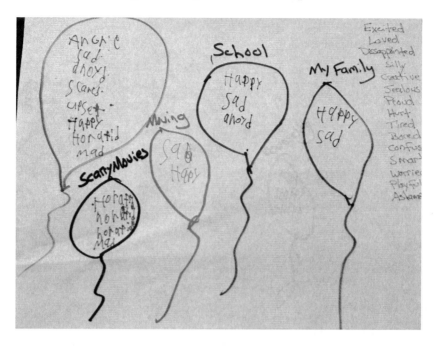

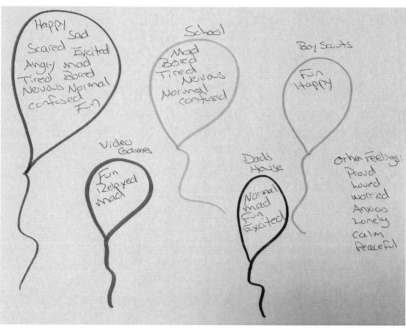

Feeling List Stop Game

Target Area	Emotional Regulation
Level	Child and Adolescent
Materials	Paper, Pencil
Modality	Individual

Introduction

The Feeling List Stop Game is a simple but effective way for children and adolescents to think about feelings, to share what makes them feel certain ways, and to communicate what they can do to help themselves feel more regulated when they are experiencing a negative feeling.

Instructions

The child is instructed to make a list of 12 feelings. (The child can look at a feelings chart or the feelings list provided in the Appendix of this book to help them identify the feelings.) The child writes the feelings on a piece of paper, down the side, numbered 1–12. (A worksheet is included here.) Once the child has completed the list, the practitioner takes the list and instructs the child that the practitioner is going to run his or her finger up and down the list without looking at the list and when the child says stop, the practitioner will stop. Whatever feeling the practitioner's finger is on, the child has to share when he or she felt that way, and if it is a negative feeling, the child has to share what he or she could do to help him or her feel better.

The practitioner may have to help the child, depending on the child's age and developmental level. When discussing a negative feeling, the practitioner and child can also role-play through any identified strategies for coping better or regulating through the negative emotion. The practitioner and child can also switch roles, and the practitioner can share his or her feelings and be a role model for the child on how to discuss feelings and ideas for handling negative feelings.

Rationale

The Feeling List Stop Game helps children and adolescents work on identifying, understanding, and expressing emotions. This technique can be played over and over again by creating new lists with new feelings. Variations can also be added, like acting out the feeling or making a feeling face. Children often enjoy switching roles with the practitioner and running his or her finger up and down the list with the practitioner sharing emotions. Parents can be taught this intervention to do at home and can be encouraged to play with their child regularly. Practitioners and parents can use the pre-created sheet included here or create their own lists.

Feeling List Stop Worksheet

1) _____

2) _____

3) _____

4) _____

5) _____

6) _____

7) _____

8) _____

9) _____

10) _____

11) _____

12) _____

Spon-Play-Ity

Target Area	Emotional Regulation
Level	Child and Adolescent
Materials	Various Playroom Toys/Games
Modality	Individual

Introduction

Children and adolescents with ASD and other developmental disorders often struggle with changes in schedule or sudden or spontaneous happenings. This intervention engages children in a playful way to practice regulating and coping when they experience sudden changes to the plan or when they experience something happening spontaneously without any warning.

Instructions

The practitioner explains to the child that they will be working on how to better handle changes to a plan or something happening without any warning. The practitioner asks the child to identify several games that he or she likes to play. The games can be traditional board games or any type of game. If the child cannot think of anything, then the practitioner should make some suggestions of games to play that the child is familiar with. The practitioner and child pick one of the identified games to start playing. After about 5 minutes, the practitioner says to the child that they are not going to play that game any longer and chooses one of the other identified games to play. The practitioner and child play the second game for about 5 minutes, and then the practitioner again stops the game and chooses a different game to play. This continues throughout most of the session. Toward the end of the session, the practitioner talks with the child about the process and asks him or her how it felt to keep changing without warning. The practitioner and child then discuss the concept of things changing from the original plan and the concept of things happening spontaneously and how the child can work on feeling OK about experiencing these changes.

Rationale

This technique helps children and adolescents work on general regulation and developing the skill of handling sudden change of plans or things that may happen without warning or preparation. The practitioner and child may want to spend some time discussing ways to stay calm when things change and try practicing those strategies during the intervention. The playful component of this intervention provides the child the opportunity to practice regulating themselves through changes in a less anxiety-stimulating context. Repetitive practice is important to help children become more comfortable with spontaneous events. The practitioner may want to implement this intervention across multiple sessions and teach parents how to implement this intervention at home.

Anxiety Buster Toolbox

Target Area	Emotional Regulation
Level	Child and Adolescent
Materials	Small Box, Art Supplies
Modality	Individual, Group

Introduction

This intervention provides a comprehensive tool for a child or adolescent to have available when he or she is feeling anxiety or dysregulated. It is likely that children with ASD will need many "tools" to choose from to help them self-calm. The Anxiety Buster Toolbox puts all the child's tools together in one accessible location where the child can choose what he or she needs to help self-calm and regulate.

Instructions

The practitioner explains to the child that they will be making a box and placing in the box several ideas for helping the child calm and regulate when he or she is feeling anxious, upset, or overwhelmed. The practitioner provides a small cardboard box for the child to decorate any way that he or she would like. The child should write his or her name somewhere on the box. Once the child has finished decorating the box, the practitioner instructs the child to cut several strips of paper. On each piece of paper, the practitioner and child will write things the child can do to help him or her calm when he or she is feeling anxiety or feeling dysregulated. The practitioner will gain feedback from the child on what he or she feels helps him or her calm but should also gain feedback, before this intervention is introduced, from the child's parents, teachers, or any other people in the child's life who may be able to identify techniques, strategies, or games that currently help the child self-calm when he or she is upset. The practitioner may also have some ideas for what might help the child and he or she can add those ideas to the box as well. Once the box is complete, the practitioner and child should practice and role-play the calming strategies.

Rationale

This technique helps children and adolescents work on decreasing anxiety, regulating, and learning strategies to help them self-calm. Anything goes in the Anxiety Buster Toolbox. Any activity, game, process, etc. that helps or may help a child self-calm can be written on a piece of paper and placed in the box. The box goes home with the child, and the child is encouraged to go to their box and find something to do to help them self-calm with they are feeling dysregulated.

Anxiety Mometer

Target Area	Emotional Regulation
Level	Child and Adolescent
Materials	Paper, Marker
Modality	Individual, Family, Group

Introduction

Children and adolescents with ASD and other developmental disorders often have difficulty differentiating between levels of dysregulation or anxiety. This intervention helps children and adolescents learn to identify different levels of dysregulation and situations or triggers that create levels of anxiety.

Instructions

The practitioner and/or child draw a thermometer outline on a piece of paper. (A thermometer template could also be used.) The practitioner and child decide on different situations to place on the thermometer with situations that create no anxiety for the child placed at the bottom of the thermometer and progressively moving up the thermometer with different situations that increasingly create more anxiety or dysregulation for the child. The practitioner and child then review all the situations and talk about interventions that the child can do at each level to help them self-calm.

The practitioner can refer to other interventions, such as the Anxiety Buster Toolbox, and write on the paper beside the thermometer different intervention ideas for the child to implement when he or she is at different levels on the thermometer. The practitioner and child can then role-play through several situations that create anxiety and practice implementing an intervention to help decrease the anxiety and dysregulation.

Rationale

This technique helps children and adolescents work on decreasing anxiety and dysregulation. This intervention provides the opportunity for children and adolescents to learn to identify when they are beginning to feel dysregulated and attend to the dysregulation before it amplifies. The practitioner should have a clear understanding of different situations that create different levels of anxiety. Practitioners may want to consult with the child's parents before completing this intervention. Children should keep the Anxiety Mometer posted at home to reference. Parents can be taught this intervention and encouraged to implement the intervention at home. Parents can also be encouraged to direct their child to their Anxiety Mometer when they notice their child becoming dysregulated and help their child implement a calming strategy.

Anxiety Mometer Examples

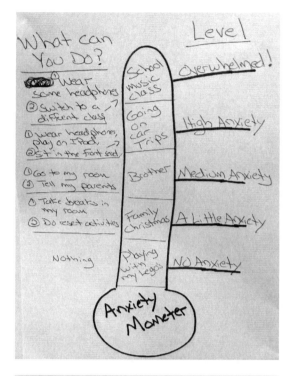

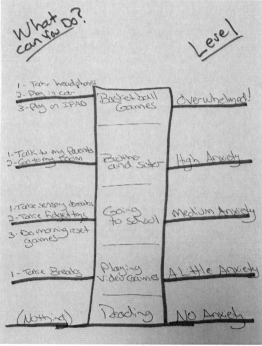

Calm Down Postcards

Target Area	Emotional Regulation
Level	Child and Adolescent
Materials	Postcards, Pencil
Materials	Individual, Group

Introduction

Children and adolescents with ASD and other developmental disorders often struggle with regulation when they are experiencing a great deal of emotion; this emotion can be both positive and negative. Calm Down Postcards help children identify situations that cause overstimulation and dysregulation and provides a cognitive, visual reminder strategy to help the child self-calm.

Instructions

This intervention can be done using real postcards or postcards the practitioner and child make out of paper. The practitioner and child write postcards to the child reminding the child to stay calm when he or she is feeling dysregulated. The postcards should address typical situations the child struggles with and a cognitive affirmation or simple self-calming activity that the child could do in the situation. The postcards can also include pictures that the child or practitioner draws to represent the self-calming activity.

The child is instructed to take the postcards home and keep them accessible so he or she will have the postcards to refer to when he or she is feeling dysregulated. The practitioner may want to consult with parents about calming strategies that seem to be successful for the child. The practitioner can also provide suggestions and practice the calming strategies with the child to identify if the strategies are helpful to the child.

Rationale

Calm Down Postcards provide children and adolescents with a visual aid that they can keep and refer to when they are feeling dysregulated. It also addresses real situations that tend to cause dysregulation for the child, so he or she can begin to conceptualize and remember strategies to help him- or herself calm during those situations. Parents can be taught this intervention and can be encouraged to make more postcards with their child. Parents can work with their child to remind him or her to refer to their postcard when they are feeling dysregulated and help their child implement the cognitive affirmation or the calming strategy.

Calm Down Postcards

Dear Me,
Today a lot of things happened at school.
Some things really upset me. Now I am home.
I can try to calm down. I can try to do my
reset activities.

Dear Me,
My mom just told me we have to go to my
brother's school play. I don't want to go.
I am feeling upset. I can try to calm down.
I can draw and paint and take my
headphones to listen to at the play.

Dear Me,
My sister just messed up my video game.
I am feeling angry and I want to hit her.
I can try to calm down. I can go tell my
parents what happened. I can punch
my punching bag.

The Always Changing Picture

Target Area	Emotional Regulation
Level	Child and Adolescent
Materials	Paper, Markers, Pencil
Modality	Individual, Family, Group

Introduction

Children and adolescents with ASD and other developmental disorders often need help in accepting transitions and managing when schedules and plans change. This intervention helps children practice handling changes in a low-stimulating environment and practice how to self-regulate when they are experiencing change.

Instructions

The practitioner explains to the child that they are going to be working on helping the child handle experiencing change. The practitioner explains that the child is going to draw a picture, but there will be changes made to the picture as the child is drawing it. The practitioner will begin by instructing the child to draw something; after a short time, the practitioner will change the instruction, giving a new instruction. The practitioner will continue to do this several times before the final drawing is complete. An example might be that the practitioner tells the child to draw a house and color the roof blue, and then halfway through the child coloring the roof blue, the practitioner changes the instruction to coloring the roof yellow. The practitioner might then instruct the child to draw a tree with leaves; as the child is drawing the leaves, the practitioner changes the instruction to no leaves. The practitioner will periodically give a new instruction, changing what was previously instructed. This provides the child with the ability to practice accepting changes without becoming dysregulated. The practitioner can be processing with and talking to the child about how he or she is feeling as changes are being presented.

Rationale

This intervention helps children and adolescents practice regulating through situations and plans that change. The goal is to help children learn to "switch gears" and stay calm in the process. By practicing in a lower-stimulating "safe" environment, the child can better prepare for real-life situations.

The practitioner should provide several changes to the original instruction so the child has several opportunities to practice regulating through change in an atmosphere that is less dysregulating. The practitioner should process with the child staying calm, regulating through changes, and applying examples to the child's real life.

5   Social Skills Interventions

Social Skills

Skill **Eye Contact** *practice*

Appropriate Friendship

Anxious **Interaction**   Expression

Social   Engaging   Joining

Body Language   *Relationship*   Connection

Reciprocal   Conversation   **Play**

Perform   *Comfort*

Friend Collage

Target Area	Social Skills
Level	Child and Adolescent
Materials	Magazines, Scissors, Glue, Paper
Modality	Individual, Group

Introduction

Children and adolescents with ASD often struggle with peer-related social skills. This intervention helps children identify what activities they could do with other children. This intervention encourages application by having the practitioner role-play scenarios with the child and establishes a "homework" assignment by asking children and adolescents to participate in one or more of the activities with another child before the next session.

Instructions

The child draws a person figure on a piece of paper. The child is then instructed to cut out from magazines several pictures and/or words of things that he or she could do or play with other children. The child glues all the cut-outs on and around the person figure drawn on the piece of paper. The child creates a collage of all the activities that he or she has identified that could be done with other children.

The practitioner and child go through each of the activities and talk about them together. The child identifies a real child who might be appropriate to do each activity with and discusses how he or she can begin to initiate completing the activity with another child. If appropriate, the practitioner and child decide on an activity that the child will try to do with a specific friend before his or her next session, and the practitioner and child can role-play the interaction.

Rationale

This technique helps children and adolescents work on social skills, specifically related to friendship skills and playing and interacting with other peers in appropriate ways. This intervention also works on helping children initiate social interactions with peers. The practitioner will need several magazines for the child to look through. Magazines that have a child focus will likely be more beneficial. If the child is struggling to identify things they can do with other children, the practitioner should help the child think of ideas. Parents can be taught to implement the intervention at home and make additional collages at home with their child. Parents can also role-play with their child and facilitate a play time for the child to practice initiating and playing one of the identified activities before the next session.

Friend Collage Examples

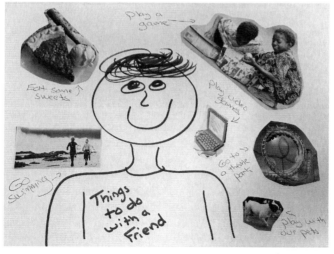

Social Scales

Target Area	Social Skills
Level	Child and Adolescent
Materials	Paper, Pencil
Modality	Individual, Group

Introduction

The Social Scales intervention is designed to help practitioners create specific scenarios in which a child or adolescent might need help in developing better or more appropriate social responses. The sample scales included here can be used or new scales can be individualized for each child. The scales provide both an assessment tool to identify what the child perceives and a practice tool to help develop social skills.

Instructions

The practitioner creates a scale sheet with several scales listed on it. The child is given an example of a situation that relates to one of the scales and the child puts an "X" on the scale where he or she believes is the correct response for the situation. The practitioner should try to create scales and situations that are relevant for skills that the child needs to develop. Once the child has given a response, the child's response should be processed with the practitioner. The practitioner should especially discuss any response that is unhealthy, unsafe, or not accurate. An example might be that the practitioner says, "A stranger walks up to you while you are at the mall or playing at a park and says if you come with me I can get you a free iPad. Mark on the scale where you think this would fall on the truth-and-lie scale and the safe-and-unsafe scale." Here are the example scales:

Truth _____ Lie

Safe _____ Unsafe

Rationale

This technique helps children and adolescents work on a variety of social skills and social situations. Scales can be directed toward identifying safety issues, giving appropriate responses, understanding concepts, etc. Once the child indicates what he or she believes, the practitioner and child should process the response and discuss if the child has responded inappropriately or if it is a situation that might have multiple correct responses. Parents can be taught this intervention at home and can be encouraged to play with their child regularly between sessions and create new scales for new situations that arise.

Social Scales Examples

You are sitting in class at school, and the boy beside you starts hitting his desk.

Appropriate _____ Not Appropriate

You are walking down the hallway at school, and another student pushes you as you pass by.

Bullying _____ Not Bullying

You meet a new student at school and talk for a few minutes about her old school.

Friend _____ Acquaintance

A student at school says your hair looks like an anime character.

Funny _____ Not Funny

You are watching a YouTube video showing a dinosaur walking in a backyard.

Fact _____ Fake

A student at school says he will be your friend if you keep his cigarettes for him.

Ok _____ Not OK

Friend _____ Not a Friend

Template

_____

Social Skills Puzzle

Target Area	Social Skills
Level	Child and Adolescent
Materials	Small Blank Puzzle, Markers, Pencil
Modality	Individual, Family, Group

Introduction

This intervention helps teach social skills to children and adolescents with ASD and other developmental disorders. The puzzle element provides a tactile and engaging element to learning specific social skills. Each puzzle is created by the practitioner and child so each puzzle is individualized to focus on skills that a particular child needs to develop.

Instructions

The practitioner explains to the child that they will be creating a puzzle that helps the child work on developing social skills. Using a small blank puzzle (6 pieces for younger children, 9 pieces for adolescents), the child writes a different social skill that he or she needs to practice on the back of each puzzle piece. On the front of the puzzle, the child can decorate the puzzle however he or she wants. For more advanced children, the child can decorate each puzzle piece to describe the social skill listed on the back side of the puzzle piece. The practitioner and child then take the puzzle apart and put it back together; each time a piece is connected, the practitioner and child practice the social skill for that puzzle piece. Children will likely have a difficult time identifying the social skills that they need to work on. The practitioner should be prepared to identify several of the social skills that will be written on the puzzle pieces.

Rationale

The Social Skills Puzzle helps children and adolescents work on a variety of social skills. This intervention provides the opportunity for children to work on specific social skills that he or she may be struggling with. The practitioner should help the child think of social skills to write on the puzzle and make sure that skills are included that the child needs to develop.

The practitioner and child can take the puzzle apart and put it back together, practicing the social skills multiple times. Parents can be taught how to implement this intervention with their children and practice the social skills puzzle several times at home. Parents and children can also make new puzzles; the puzzles can be put together, and social skills can be practiced with other family members. Blank puzzles can be ordered several places online including at Amazon.com.

Social Skills Puzzle

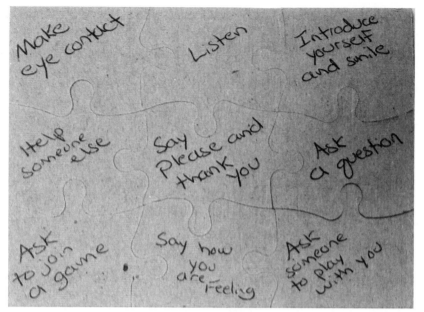

(Back: Nine identified social skills to practice)

(Front: A picture representation of each identified social skill)

Let's Practice Conversation

Target Area	Social Skills
Level	Child and Adolescent
Materials	None
Modality	Individual

Introduction

Children and adolescents with social skill deficits often have trouble entering and maintaining a conversation. Individuals with ASD often report struggling with "small talk" and knowing what to say and how to participate in a social conversation. This intervention helps children practice the various components of being in a reciprocal conversation.

Instructions

The practitioner gives instruction to the child that they are going to practice being in a reciprocal conversation. The practitioner gives the following instruction for how the conversation is going to flow back and forth: The practitioner is going to ask the child a question. The child is going to answer the question in a succinct way, avoiding going off on a tangent, and at the same time, avoiding giving a one-word answer. Once the child is done answering the question, the child will then ask the practitioner a question back. The child will listen to the practitioner's answer and when the practitioner is done, the child has to repeat back to the practitioner what the practitioner said. This process is repeated several times for practice.

Rationale

Let's Practice Conversation helps children and adolescents work on social skills, specifically conversation skills, which include asking questions, staying focused in conversations, avoiding talking too much, avoiding going off on tangents, participating in "small talk," and listening to others. This intervention should be practiced many times; the more a child can participate in this intervention, the better he or she will become in participating in conversations.

It is likely the child will not do well in the beginning and that the practitioner will have to stop the intervention several times and give prompts to help keep the child focused and participating correctly. Parents can be taught how to do this intervention at home with the expectation of practicing several times with their child. After several practices, parents can also arrange real-life situations where the child can engage in reciprocal conversations.

Candy Questions

Target Area	Social Skills
Level	Child and Adolescent
Materials	Candy
Modality	Individual, Group

Introduction

Children with ASD often struggle with simply asking and answering questions, especially in a public setting. This intervention helps children and adolescents work on fully answering another person's questions and asking other people questions. The candy serves as a reinforcement to help keep the child engaged.

Instructions

The practitioner chooses a candy that contains several pieces, such as a bag of Skittles. The practitioner should try to choose a candy that the child likes and also consider if the child has any special diet restrictions. If the child cannot eat candy, the practitioner should use something like stickers or pennies as a substitute. The practitioner tells the child they are going to play Candy Questions. The practitioner is going to ask the child an open-ended question, and the child has to fully answer the question, and if the child does this, he or she will receive a piece of candy. The child then has to ask the practitioner a question, the practitioner will answer, and the child receives a piece of candy for asking a question. This exchange goes back and forth until the candy is gone or the practitioner ends the intervention.

Rationale

This technique helps children and adolescents work on social skills, specifically conversation skills, which include asking and answering questions. It would be beneficial for the practitioner to have a predetermined set of questions written out to ask the child. Questions should be designed to relate to real issues or things happening in the child's life. If candy is not acceptable for the child, something like stickers or pennies would be alternatives.

The practitioner should try to practice with the child several times to gain skill development. Parents can be taught this intervention and should practice at home with their child several times between counseling sessions. Parents should be strongly encouraged to practice as often as possible because the more the child practices, the more improvement he or she will gain in conversation skills, becoming more confident and comfortable asking and answering questions.

Friend Mapping

Target Area	Social Skills
Level	Child and Adolescent
Materials	Friend Mapping Worksheet
Modality	Individual

Introduction

Children and adolescents with ASD and other developmental disorders typically have a hard time understanding friendships and differentiating friends from acquaintances. This intervention helps children better identify what friendship looks like and serves as an assessment tool to help the practitioner gain a better understanding of what is happening in regard to the child's peer relationships.

Instructions

The practitioner tells the child that they are going to work on discussing and identifying friendships. Using the Friend Mapping Worksheet (included here), the child is instructed to complete each section. In the circles, the child will write 3 current friends, 3 things he or she does with friends, 3 things the child does with other children of the same age, and 3 people that he or she would like to be friends with. In the 2 rectangles, the child will write 2 things that are good friendship skills. The practitioner will then process through the map with the child asking follow-up questions to gain a better understating of the child's current reality and perceptions of friendships. If the child is struggling to identify any areas of the Friendship Map, the practitioner should provide assistance to the child.

Rationale

Friend Mapping is an intervention that helps children and adolescents work on social skills, specifically skills related to peer relationships and friendships. Children with ASD often need help in differentiating among relationship levels and help in creating and participating in friendships. This intervention also serves as an assessment tool for practitioners to gain a more clear understanding of the child's current friendship functioning and the child's perception of what constitutes a friend.

Practitioners will likely begin and end this intervention with a discussion of what friendship actually looks like. It is likely the practitioner will have to help the child clearly understand and discriminate between the people he or she is referring to as friends. Often children with ASD consider acquaintances close friends and struggle to actually engage in deeper friendship relationships.

Friend Mapping Worksheet

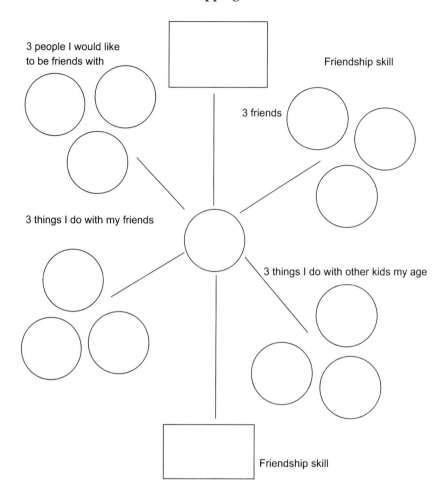

What Am I?

Target Area	Social Skills
Level	Child and Adolescent
Materials	Index Cards, Tape, Pencil
Modality	Individual, Family, Group

Introduction

Children and adolescents with ASD can struggle with basic social skills such as making eye contact and asking questions. This intervention helps children and adolescents work on asking other people questions and maintaining focus, attention, and eye contact. This intervention presents a fun and engaging way to work on developing these social skills.

Instructions

The practitioner explains to the child that they will be playing a game that works on increasing social skills. On index cards, the practitioner writes several different things, such as types of food, animals, toys, material objects, etc. There should be a variety of items, and one item is written on each index card. (The cards should be created prior to the child coming in for a session.) The index cards should be placed on the floor with the writing face down. The child and practitioner each choose one card and put a small piece of tape on the blank side and tape the card to their chests without looking at what is written on it. The practitioner and child then take turns asking the other questions to try and discover what is written on the index card taped on their chest.

The child and practitioner have to maintain eye contact when asking and answering questions and cannot look down at what is written on the index card taped to their chest. When someone accurately guesses what is written on his or her index card, then he or she can put tape on another card and continue with the process until all the cards have been guessed or the practitioner ends the intervention.

Rationale

This technique helps children and adolescents work on social skills, specifically asking questions, answering questions, and making eye contact. The practitioner should create at least 10 cards to go through in playing the intervention. New cards can be created, and the game can be played multiple times. Parents can be taught this intervention and encouraged to play regularly at home with their child. Parents can also involve other family members and the entire family can play together.

What Am I?

Stepping Stones

Target Area	Social Skills
Level	Child and Adolescent
Materials	Card Stock, Foam Pieces, Sharpie, Small Prize
Modality	Individual, Family, Group

Introduction

Children and adolescents with ASD and other developmental disorders often have a difficult time understanding appropriate versus inappropriate behaviors in various social situations or contexts. This intervention creates a game format that can be played repeatedly so children can practice appropriate behaviors for a variety of settings.

Instructions

The child cuts out 6–8 pieces of foam in the shape of stepping stones. The foam pieces are then glued on a piece of card stock to form a path with a designated beginning and end. The practitioner and child then decide on various situations the child is typically in and write a situation on each stepping stone. The child can then decorate the rest of the card stock in any way he or she wants, and on the last stepping stone, the child should write "PRIZE!"

The practitioner and child then play the Stepping Stones game. The child starts at the first stone and reads the situation. The child then has to talk about and act out an inappropriate behavior and an appropriate behavior that could be done in that situation. The child then moves on to the second stone and repeats the process until he or she gets to the end and receives a small prize, such as a small toy, sticker, or piece of candy.

Rationale

The Stepping Stones game helps children and adolescents work on social skills, specifically inappropriate and appropriate behaviors for various situations, such as sitting in a classroom, waiting in a doctor's office, being in a grocery store, eating at the dinner table, etc. Situations that tend to be struggle situations for the child should be chosen for the game. Practitioners may want to consult with parents and other individuals involved in the child's life to collect a variety of situations that the child typically struggles with or displays inappropriate behavior in. The practitioner should ask the child to identify situations and scenarios, but the practitioner should make sure that the game includes several situations that are known problem areas for the child. The game goes home with the child, and parents are taught to play the game with their child and encouraged to play regularly between counseling sessions. Parents and child can even create a new game with different situations.

Stepping Stones

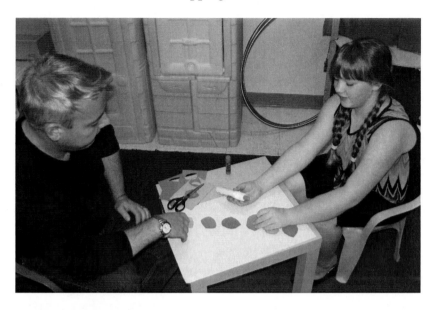

Symbolic Play Time

Target Area	Social Skills
Level	Child
Materials	Various Toys
Modality	Individual

Introduction

Children with ASD typically struggle with pretend and symbolic play skills. Often children with ASD find themselves in peer situations where pretend play is the most common form of play, and thus, children with ASD struggle to engage with and participate in pretend play with their peers. This intervention helps children practice and learn how to engage in symbolic and pretend play.

Instructions

The practitioner instructs the child that they are going to have some pretend play time. The practitioner explains the concept of pretend and symbolic play and introduces the child to some toys that will be used in the pretend play time. The practitioner should use nondescript toys such as blocks. The practitioner tells the child they are going to pick a block and give it a name and a character, such as making it a made-up person or an animal. The child gets to choose the name and the character of the block he or she picks, and the practitioner does the same. The practitioner then instructs that they are going to make up a pretend story using their 2 block people/animals. The practitioner begins by having the 2 blocks interacting in a short simple story. Then, the practitioner begins incorporating the child into the decision making. The practitioner will continue on with the play interaction, trying to involve the child as much as possible. The practitioner can periodically switch to different toys and create other symbolic play interactions.

Rationale

This technique helps children work on social and play skills, specifically symbolic or pretend play skills, which are often a component of social interactions with same-age peers. Practitioners can vary the symbolic play time using different toys and creating different scenarios. The practitioner will likely have to take the lead in directing the pretend play but should always be looking for opportunities to have the child make decisions and engage in a leading way in the pretend play. This intervention can be played several times and will typically be implemented over the span of several sessions to try and help the child better understand symbolic play.

Paper Friend

Target Area	Social Skills
Level	Child and Adolescent
Materials	White Paper, Construction Paper, Scissors, Glue
Modality	Individual, Group

Introduction

Children and adolescents with ASD often desire to have friends but lack the social skills to establish and maintain friendships. This intervention helps children work on specific friendship-related skills, on targeting children to engage with, and on strategies to develop friendships.

Instructions

The practitioner explains to the child that they will be working on increasing friendship skills. The practitioner or child draws an outline of a person on a white piece of paper. The child identifies someone in his or her life that he or she would like to be friends with. The child designs the person outline to look like the child he or she would like to be friends with (typically by drawing the identified child's face on the paper outline person). The child then writes things on the person outline that he or she could do with that person, things they could talk about, ways that he or she could be good friends to that person, ways that he or she could initiate with that person, skills that help make friends, and what would make that person a good friend. The practitioner and child process through what the child has written, and the practitioner may add additional information. The practitioner and child then practice the various friendship-related skills through role-play. The practitioner will likely have to help the child identify friendship skills.

Rationale

This technique helps children and adolescents work on social skills, specifically related to making and keeping friends. The child can make several Paper Friends for several different children that the child knows and would like to be friends with. The practitioner and child can also practice the child introducing himself or herself to the potential friend and the initial steps in getting to know someone along with the ideas that have been written on the Paper Friend. Parents can be taught this intervention, encouraged to practice the skills at home, and encouraged to try to arrange opportunities for the child to connect with the child he or she would like to become friends with or another appropriate child.

Paper Friend Examples

Instruction Puzzle

Target Area	Social Skills
Level	Child and Adolescent
Materials	Small Blank Puzzle, Marker
Modality	Individual, Group

Introduction

The Instruction Puzzle provides an engaging way to create a visual task schedule for children and adolescents with ASD. The puzzle pieces serve as steps to complete, and the puzzle can be completed as the child accomplished each of the steps.

Instructions

The practitioner will give the child a small blank puzzle, probably no larger than 6 pieces for a young child and 9 for an adolescent. On the front of each puzzle piece, the practitioner and child will write instructions, broken down in steps, toward completing something. The practitioner and child will decide on something to instruct about, such as how to create a Facebook account, steps to brushing your teeth, a morning routine, or how to check out a book at the library. (A task or activity should be chosen that the child actually struggles with or does not know how to do.) The child will try to write on the front of each puzzle piece (going in order) steps to accomplish or complete the task. The child can also add pictures to describe each step. The practitioner should allow the child to complete as much of the instruction puzzle as he or she can and the practitioner can assist the child as needed.

Once instructions/steps have been written on all the puzzle pieces and the instructions are complete, the practitioner and child put the puzzle together in the appropriate order for each step to complete the task. The practitioner and child take turns picking a piece of the puzzle and explain or teach that instruction to the other until the whole puzzle is complete. The practitioner and child can practice completing the task several times.

Rationale

This technique helps children and adolescents work on social skills, specifically teaching and giving instructions to others and learning how to complete different tasks that are relevant to the child. It also serves as a visual task-completing schedule for the child. Several puzzles can be made to address several different tasks. It is helpful if the tasks are actual things the child needs to learn to complete. The puzzle should be sent home, and parents can be taught how to use the puzzle with their child to complete the identified task.

Instruction Puzzle

(Child identifying steps in a morning routine)

(Adolescent giving instructions for getting a driver's license)

Bully in the Way

Target Area	Social Skills
Level	Child and Adolescent
Materials	White Paper, Markers, Small Prize
Modality	Individual

Introduction

Children and adolescents with ASD and other developmental disorders are typically more susceptible to being victims of bullying than neurotypical peers. This intervention helps children role-play and practice what to do and what to say if someone is trying to bully them.

Instructions

The practitioner explains to the child that they are going to discuss ways to address bullying behavior. The practitioner and child draw and cut out several people shapes. The child decorates each people shape to represent a real person who has bullied the child. (If the child cannot think of real people then generic bullies can be used.) Once the child is finished, each of the "bullies" is placed on the floor scattered from one side of the room to the other side. The practitioner discusses with the child how each person the child made has bullied him or her. The child then starts at one side of the room, walks up to each bully, confronts that bully, and practices a healthy response or action that he or she could give to that bully. (The practitioner will have to teach the child various responses or actions that the child could take, some examples are included here.) The child confronts each bully one at a time until he or she gets through all the bullies and is on the other side of the room. After the last bully has been confronted, the child receives a small prize provided by the practitioner.

Rationale

This technique helps children and adolescents work on social skills specifically related to addressing and handling bullying. The practitioner will likely have to help the child learn healthy ways to confront bullies and teach the child different options for responding to bullies. The practitioner may also need to discuss bullying problems with parents who may need to contact the school if bullying is happening at school and make the school administration aware of the bullying. Both parents and school officials may need to be involved in eliminating the bullying and in knowing what approaches the child is trying to implement when he or she is bullied. A list of web resources for addressing bullying is included here.

Bully in the Way

Example Interventions to Teach Children

Tell the school counselor or teacher

Tell your parents

Teach comeback phrases

Teach positive cognition statements to say to self

Leave the situation

Teach self-worth concepts to improve self-esteem

Talk loudly back to the bully

Call the bully by their name and tell them to stop

Stand up straight and look the bully in the eye

Stay with friends

Ignore the bully

Make kind statements back

Make a joke about what the bully said

Keep a journal of the bullying

Act shocked and then give the bully a compliment

Teach "I" messages: I don't like it when_____, stop!

Work with the school to create a peer assignment program

(Bullying resources)

www.schoolviolencehotline.com

www.stopbullying.gov

www.bullyfree.com

www.pacer.org

www.nasponline.org

www.nea.org

www.safekids.com

www.violencepreventionworks.org

Social Media

Target Area	Social Skills
Level	Adolescent
Materials	Computer, Social Media Account
Modality	Individual, Group

Introduction

Social media sites are very popular among adolescents and many adolescents with ASD and developmental disorders lack the social skills to navigate social media sites. This intervention teaches adolescents how to identify appropriate and inappropriate ways to use social media sites and how to stay safe with their interactions.

Instructions

The practitioner tells the adolescent that they will be discussing appropriate ways to use social media. The practitioner and adolescent discuss the various social media options including Facebook. (Practitioners should discuss with parents if the child currently has any social media accounts and/or if they are planning to allow the child to have one before implementing this intervention.) The following acronym is written down on a piece of paper:

F = friends
A = angry
C = careful
E = embarrassing
B = bad
O = odd
O = oh no!
K = kind

The practitioner and child discuss what different Facebook posts would look like for each of the above categories, for example, "Who is a friend?" "Why is that person a friend?" "What is an angry post?" "Is it appropriate to post angry things?" "What would be an embarrassing post?" "What would be an odd or bad to post?" "What is a post that could get someone in trouble?" and "What is a kind or appropriate post?" The practitioner and child try to find examples of each one on the child's or practitioner's Facebook newsfeed.

Rationale

This technique helps adolescents work on social skills related to participating in and socializing through social media. This technique requires the child to have a social media account or permission from parents to develop one. Parents should monitor the child's social media account and practice this intervention periodically at home with their child.

I'm Going

Target Area	Social Skills
Level	Child and Adolescent
Materials	Index Cards
Modality	Individual, Family, Group

Introduction

Children and adolescents with ASD typically need practice in regard to learning social skills and appropriate ways to respond or behave in certain situations. The I'm Going intervention helps children and adolescents identify struggle situations and practice an appropriate behavior or response for that situation.

Instructions

The practitioner explains to the child that they are going to play a game to practice appropriate responses for certain situations. The practitioner writes various I'm Going situations on index cards. Example situations could include "I'm going to school," "I'm going to an amusement park," "I'm going to a restaurant," "I'm going to a friend's house," "I'm going to church," and "I'm going to the doctor." (Sample cards are included here.) The index cards are placed face down in a pile, and the child and practitioner take turns drawing the cards. The child should go first. When a card is drawn, both the practitioner and the child each say something that is an appropriate social skill that he or she will do where he or she is going. For example, if the "I am going to school" card is drawn, the child might say, "I am going to school, and I am going to listen when the teacher is talking." Then the practitioner might say, "I am going to school, and I am going to wait in line when it is recess time." The practitioner should try to write 8–10 situations on index cards. The situations should be real situations that the child would participate in and may be having struggles in displaying appropriate behavior.

Rationale

This technique helps children and adolescents work on social skills, specifically related to appropriate behaviors in certain situations. The practitioner should make sure that the child provides an appropriate response. If the child cannot think of a response or provides an inappropriate response, the practitioner should explain an appropriate response to the child. The practitioner can add an extra element to this intervention by role-playing the appropriate behavior after the child and practitioner have given a response. Parents can be taught this intervention and the entire family can play at home.

I'm Going Card Set

I'm going to school.	I'm going to a restaurant.	I'm going to the doctor's office.
I'm going to get my hair cut.	I'm going to a friend's house.	I'm going to church.
I'm going to the grocery store.	I'm going for a ride in the car.	I'm going to a party.
I'm going to the dentist office.	I'm going to the shoe store.	I'm going to a park.
I'm going to the mall.	I'm going for a walk.	I'm going to the post office.

Interview Me

Target Area	Social Skills
Level	Child and Adolescent
Materials	Paper, Pencil
Modality	Individual, Family, Group

Introduction

This intervention helps children and adolescents work on social skills related to talking to others, asking others questions, and learning about others. It also helps children and adolescents stay focused and avoid talking excessively about a particular fixation topic and going off topic during a conversation.

Instructions

The child is instructed that he or she is going to interview the practitioner. The child is given a piece of paper and a pencil and asked to come up with 7 questions to ask the practitioner. The questions need to be open-ended questions, avoiding yes-or-no response questions. The child should try to come up with the questions, but if he or she is struggling, then the practitioner can offer the example worksheet included here. Once the child has written his or her questions, then he or she will ask them to the practitioner, listen to the practitioner's answers, and write the responses down. The guidelines for the child are that he or she cannot wander into a tangent or talk about him- or herself and he or she needs to try to listen to the practitioner's answers. The practitioner and child discuss the interview and if the child was able to follow the guidelines. The practitioner and child can practice through several interviews if there is time. The child is then instructed to go home and interview 3 people in the same format, using the same guidelines, and bring the interviews to the next session. The practitioner and child will then discuss how the home interviews went.

Rationale

This technique helps children and adolescents work on social skills related to asking others questions, listening, and staying focused in a conversation. The child may struggle with coming up with appropriate interview questions and may struggle with getting through the interview in an appropriate manner. At any point, the practitioner can stop the intervention and help the child stay focused and follow the guidelines. It will likely take practice for the child to complete this intervention without help from the practitioner. Parents should be made aware that the child is going to do 3 interviews at home and assist their child in completing the assignment.

Interview Me Worksheet

1. What is your name?

    _____

    _____

2. What is one of your favorite things to do?

    _____

    _____

3. Where would you like to go on vacation and why?

    _____

    _____

4. Why do you think school is important?

    _____

    _____

5. Tell me about a time you got angry.

    _____

    _____

6. Tell me about a good family memory.

    _____

    _____

7. What do you do to calm down when you feel anxious?

    _____

    _____

That Does Not Sound the Way It Looks

Target Area	Social Skills
Level	Child and Adolescent
Materials	None
Modality	Individual

Introduction

That Does Not Sound the Way It Looks intervention helps children and adolescents work on recognizing body language and listening to what others are saying. Further, it helps children and adolescents navigate to a more accurate understanding and meaning when observing and listening to others.

Instructions

The practitioner tells the child that they are going to practice identifying situations when communicating with others and the interaction is not making sense. The practitioner is going to say something like "I am happy" in an angry voice with angry body language. The child has to say what does not make sense about what the practitioner presented. For example, the child would say, "Your face and the sound of your voice did not seem happy even though you said you were happy." Some other examples the practitioner might give include saying "I am sad" with a happy face and upbeat body language or saying "I really like going to the park" with a sad face and sad tone of voice. The practitioner should have several examples prepared before the session with the child. The practitioner can also ask the child if he or she would like to create some examples and have the practitioner identify what does not make sense.

Rationale

Children and adolescents with ASD often have struggles with understanding and accurately identifying other people's body language and understating their intention by what they say. They also struggle with their own presentation and communicating with their words and body language what they are thinking and feeling. This technique helps children and adolescents work on social skills, specifically recognizing and accurately reading body language on others, recognizing others emotions, and recognizing and identifying changes in tone of voice. Parents can be taught how to implement this intervention and encouraged to play at home with their child.

Tweet, Tweet, Tweet

Target Area	Social Skills
Level	Adolescent
Materials	Paper, Pencil, Example Tweets
Modality	Individual, Group

Introduction

Adolescents with ASD are typically exposed to social media and often have a difficult time navigating appropriateness in social situations especially through a media format. This intervention helps adolescents practice what appropriate and inappropriate social media responses look like on social media sites.

Instructions

The practitioner explains to the adolescent that they will be discussing appropriate and inappropriate social media comments. The practitioner and child then role-play sending appropriate and inappropriate messages back and forth to each other. The child should be able to identify the appropriate from the inappropriate and why the inappropriate messages are considered inappropriate. The practitioner then gives the adolescent several real tweets taken from Twitter (several are included here), and the adolescent has to put them in 2 piles: One pile is for appropriate tweets, and the other pile is for inappropriate tweets. The child has to talk about why they think each tweet is either appropriate or inappropriate. If the adolescent is unsure if the tweet is appropriate or inappropriate, then he or she can make a third pile of unsure tweets, and the practitioner and adolescent can further discuss those tweets. The practitioner should provide feedback and assist the child if he or she is not correctly labeling tweets.

Rationale

This technique helps adolescents work on social skills, specifically skills related to participating in and socializing through social media. This intervention does not require the adolescent to have a Twitter or any other social media account. It is a good intervention to practice before a child actually acquires any social media account. The practitioner should discuss with parents the relevance of social media access in the adolescent's life before implementing this intervention. If the adolescent is currently using any social media site or is planning to, this would be an appropriate intervention to implement. This intervention can be taught to parents at home, and parents can continue to implement this intervention periodically with their adolescent.

Example Tweets

Real Tweets Posted on Twitter

Develop an attitude of #gratitude and give thanks for everything that happens to you.

Lol no one likes you.

MERRY CHRISTMAS to the members and families of the Ozark Drumline!

Friday afternoon will be warm and sunny; colder weekend.

so are you straight or gay I'm like really confused.

F#%k my mom she deletes my fb dat b#%*h can go die.

I hate you, Ted.

You and me. Lunch next week. I won't be late this time.

that's like saying Superman is better than Batman. You're dead to me.

Just finished doing laundry ☺ I hate Laundry!

Congratulations! Your new baby is so cute!!!!!

This is a great website for information on bully prevention.

She is a complete slut! I hate her!!! HATE!!!

I am seriously going to kill someone if all these a#%es don't stop messing with me.

The Hobbit is an awesome movie! Just saw it—Loved It!

Really frustrated with everything right now.

I love Justin Beiber, if you say anything bad about him I will kill you—you stupid idiot!

Guess who is on TV acting like a total retard!?!

The #MSUBears defeated Alabama A&M, 68–47. Pickens posted a 15-rebound effort in the win.

Finals are over getting DRUNK tonight!

Home alone, so bored. Somebody hit me up!

Role-Play

Target Area	Social Skills
Level	Child and Adolescent
Materials	None
Modality	Individual, Family, Group

Introduction

Children and adolescents with ASD and other developmental disorders benefit greatly from role-playing through situations. Practitioners have the ability to identify several situations where a child or adolescent may need to improve their social functioning or their behaviors. Role-playing should be about the child and his or her situation and real situations the child struggles with. Role-plays can be fun and engaging and can include props and other people.

Instructions

The practitioner explains to the child that they are going to role-play some situations the child has been struggling with. The practitioner and child will decide on various social situations to role-play and social skills to work on during the role-plays. Some typical examples include recognizing when someone does something on purpose or accident, how to act when winning and losing, when to talk and when to listen, how to ask a teacher a question, saying hello and goodbye, how to respond to a bully, etc. Role-plays should be practiced several times throughout a session. Repetition and practice are essential for skill acquisition. The more the child can role-play situations and behaviors, the more likely he or she will be able to implement the desired behaviors during a real situation.

Rationale

This technique helps develop social skills through a role-play. The practitioner and child can work on a whole variety of social skills. One of the best ways to work on social skill development for children with ASD is through role-play. The practitioner can pick any scenario; role-play through it with the child; and cover how to act, respond, or handle the situation. When doing a role-play, it is best to avoid working in metaphors or in an approximation to the child's situation; instead, focus should be on directly talking about the child and what he or she should do in a situation. Role-plays can be taught to parents, and parents can practice the role-plays at home with their child. Parents can also role-play any situation that comes up that they feel needs attention. Some more common examples that a child with ASD might need to practice include how to act in a restaurant, using your manners, how to act in the car, what to do when your sibling makes you mad, doing chores, etc.

Common Role-Play Scenarios

Recognizing when someone does something on purpose or by accident

How to respond when winning and losing

When to talk and when to listen

How to ask a teacher a question

Saying "hello" and "goodbye"

How to behave in a restaurant

How to order your own food in a restaurant

Saying "please" and "thank you"

How to behave in the car

What to do when your sibling makes you mad

How to behave when your parents ask you to do some chores

How to behave when standing in line and waiting for something

Different tones of voice for different situations

How to behave when you are getting your hair cut

How to behave when you are in the doctor's office

Making eye contact when talking to someone

How to behave at the dinner table

How to take care of a pet

How to play with other children

Understanding appropriateness with humor

Roll of the Dice

Target Area	Social Skills
Level	Child and Adolescent
Materials	6 Dice, Paper, Pencil
Modality	Individual, Family, Group

Introduction

The Roll of the Dice intervention gives the practitioner the ability to practice specific social skills that the child or adolescent is struggling with and needs to improve upon. The dice provide a fun way for the child to engage and participate in practicing social skills. The child can participate in thinking about and deciding what skills he or she believes he or she needs to improve.

Instructions

The practitioner explains to the child that they are going to play a game and practice some social skills that the child needs to improve. On a piece of paper, the practitioner and child write down 6 social skills that the child needs to practice and label them 1 through 6. The practitioner should let the child try to think of some social skills that he or she feels need improvement. If the child cannot think of any, the practitioner should write down social skills that the practitioner knows the child needs to develop. The child will then roll 6 small dice, pick one of the numbers rolled, and practice the matching numbered social skill. After the child has practiced that social skill, one of the dice will be removed, and the child will roll 5 dice and again pick one of the numbers rolled and practice the matching numbered social skill. This will continue until all 6 social skills have been chosen and practiced. The practitioner role-plays and practices each social skill with the child. After all 6 social skills have been practiced, the practitioner and child can play the game again or create 6 new social skills and play the game again addressing the new social skills. The practitioner should try to make the game fun and engaging for the child. The practitioner can incorporate props such as hats, masks, toys, etc., to try make the social skill practice more enjoyable.

Rationale

This technique helps children and adolescents work on social skills. The social skills addressed can be anything that the child or adolescent needs to improve. This intervention allows the practitioner the flexibility to target any social skill that the child needs to develop. It is important to allow the child to identify social skills that he or she believes need improvement, but the practitioner should make sure that skills listed on the paper are skills the child needs to practice and develop. Parents can be taught how to do this intervention at home and can be encouraged to play with the entire family. The skills can be changed each time the activity is played.

Roll of the Dice

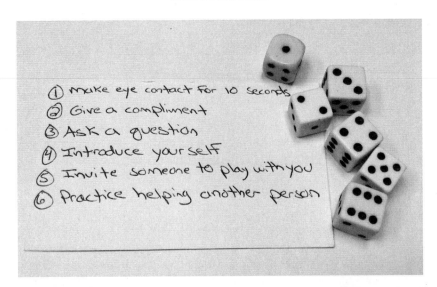

① make eye contact for 10 seconds
② Give a compliment
③ Ask a question
④ Introduce yourself
⑤ Invite someone to play with you
⑥ Practice helping another person

Social Media Friend, Foe, or Other

Target Area	Social Skills
Level	Adolescent
Materials	Social Media Account, Index Cards, Pencil
Modality	Individual, Group

Introduction

Adolescents with ASD and other developmental disorders are often attracted to engaging with other people though social media as it provides a safe boundary and usually presents less social anxiety. This intervention helps adolescents understand different levels of knowing someone and what it means to know someone in person versus through a social media site. It also opens up the discussion of what it looks like to be safe and cautious when using social media sites.

Instructions

The practitioner explains to the adolescent that they are going to discuss being safe when interacting with others through social media. This intervention requires that the adolescent have a social media account. The practitioner should discuss this intervention with parents before implementing it with the adolescent. The practitioner and adolescent go through the adolescent's friend or followers list on one of the adolescent's social media accounts. The adolescent identifies each person as a friend, a family member, an acquaintance, a stranger, or an enemy and tells the practitioner if he or she knows the person in real life or through social media. As the adolescent identifies, the practitioner writes the name down on an index card, how the adolescent labels the person and if the adolescent knows the person in real life or through social media. After each person has been covered, all the index cards are placed in categories according to how the adolescent identified the person. The practitioner and adolescent then go through each category and talk about the number of "friends" in that category and the number of people the adolescent knows only through social media. The practitioner and adolescent then discuss different levels of knowing people and the appropriateness of interacting through social media with people that are only known online and how to be safe in those interactions.

Rationale

This technique helps adolescents work on social skills related to participating in and socializing through social media. This intervention also works on understanding different levels of knowing people and what constitutes a "friend." Parents should monitor social media accounts and be taught this technique to do at home with their child periodically.

Social Skills Fortune Tellers

Target Area	Social Skills
Level	Child and Adolescent
Materials	Paper, Marker
Modality	Individual, Family, Group

Introduction

The Social Skills Fortune Tellers intervention provides a fun and engaging game for children to practice social skills. The social skills chosen should apply to the child and be skills that the child and practitioner can practice together. The tactile and movement piece of the fortune teller provides an engaging and regulating component for the child. Fine motor skills are also practiced in this intervention.

Instructions

The practitioner explains to the child that they are going to be making paper fortune tellers and using the fortune tellers to practice social skills. The practitioner teaches the child how to make a fortune teller out of white paper or colored construction paper (instructions for the creation of the fortune teller are included here). Fortune tellers should have numbers on the outside, colors on the inside, and social skills written on the tab on the other side of the colors. After the fortune teller has been created, the practitioner and child can take turns playing the game. The basic process of the game is as follows: The practitioner holds the fortune teller in his or her fingers. The child chooses a number, and the practitioner moves the fortune teller back and forth the number of times for the number the child chose. The practitioner opens up the fortune teller, and the child chooses a color. The practitioner lifts the tab for that color, which reveals a social skill. The practitioner and child then practice that social skill. The practitioner and child will decide on various social skills to write on the inside of the fortune teller. The practitioner should let the child try to come up with some social skills, but the practitioner will likely have to help and should make sure social skills are chosen that the child needs to develop. There will be 8 social skills written inside the fortune teller.

Rationale

This technique helps children and adolescents work on social skills. This intervention provides the opportunity to work on several social skills. The practitioner should direct the social skills toward skills that the child needs to develop. More than one fortune teller can be made. The child and practitioner may make several, all with different social skills to work on. The child can take their fortune tellers home and play with other family members. Parents are taught how to make fortune tellers at home and taught how to play the game with their children.

Instructions for playing the Fortune Teller game: The outer layer is numbers; the practitioner holds the fortune teller, and the child picks a number. The practitioner moves the fortune teller back and forth that many numbers and opens up the fortune teller. The inside is colors; the child picks a color, and the practitioner pulls up that color and reads the social skill underneath that color. The practitioner and child practice/role-play the social skill together.

Fortune Tellers Examples

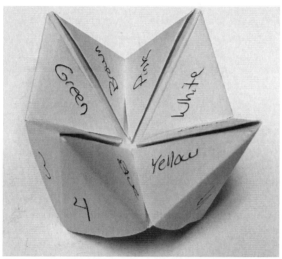

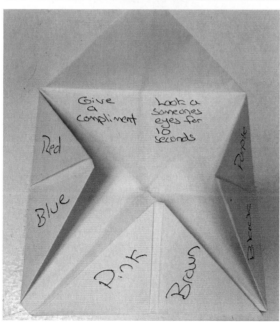

Take It to the Judge

Target Area	Social Skills
Level	Adolescent
Materials	None
Modality	Individual

Introduction

Adolescents with ASD and other developmental disorders often have thoughts and beliefs about themselves and the world around them that are not accurate and tend to produce anxiety, worry, and avoidance behaviors for the adolescent. Many of these beliefs are driven by poor social skills resulting in negative or poor social experiences. Take It to the Judge is an intervention that helps adolescents challenge their inaccurate thoughts and beliefs.

Instructions

This intervention is often implemented after the practitioner has developed rapport with the adolescent and has an understanding about what irrational or inaccurate beliefs the adolescent might be having. The practitioner makes a list of some of the inaccurate thoughts and presents the list to the adolescent. The adolescent chooses one to begin with. The practitioner explains they are going to take this thought to the "Judge" who will be played by the practitioner. The adolescent will be the attorney for both sides arguing to the judge why the thought is accurate and arguing to the judge why the thought is not accurate. The adolescent gets a few minutes to prepare what he or she wants to say. The adolescent then presents both sides to the practitioner. The practitioner addresses what is presented and makes a verdict. The practitioner should talk with the adolescent about any irrational or inaccurate thoughts or beliefs the adolescent is holding. The practitioner should try to present evidence that the thought is inaccurate and try to move the adolescent away from the inaccurate thought with a more accurate one.

Rationale

This intervention helps adolescents address any irrational or inaccurate thought that might be driving negative emotions or withdrawn behavior. The practitioner wants to use rational, concrete information to help the adolescent see any inaccurate thought. The process is repeated for all the identified inaccurate thoughts until all have been addressed. This intervention is cognitive based and provides a fun and engaging way to address inaccurate thoughts and beliefs.

Three Foam Dice

Target Area	Social Skills
Level	Child and Adolescent
Materials	Foam Dice, Marker
Modality	Individual, Family, Group

Introduction

Three Foam Dice is an intervention that focuses on preventative practice to help children avoid getting into a dysregulated state. This intervention incorporates working on increasing social skills, on increasing emotional regulation ability, and on improving relationship development.

Instructions

Using 3 foam dice (see picture included here), the practitioner designates one of the die to be social skills, one to be emotions, and one to be connection activities. The practitioner then writes a social skill to practice on each side of the social skills die, a different emotion on each side of the emotions die, and a connection activity on each side of the connection die. The information that the practitioner writes should correspond to the individual child or adolescent's specific challenges. The practitioner will usually create the dice before the child's session. The child rolls all 3 dice, and whatever is displayed on the upside of each dice is what the child has to do and the number of times that he or she has to do it. For example, if the child rolls the emotions die and rolls a number 3 and the emotion written on that side is sad, the child has to share 3 things that have made him or her feel sad. If he or she rolled a number 4 on the social skills die, and give someone a compliment was written on that side, then the child would have to give 4 compliments. If he or she rolled a 1 on the connection die, and shake someone's hand was written on that side, then the child would shake someone's hand once. The practitioner and child continue to roll the dice and play the intervention until they have implemented everything written on the dice or until the practitioner ends the game.

Rationale

The Three Foam Dice intervention works on multiple issues simultaneously. Social skills, emotional regulation, and connection challenges can all be covered in this intervention. When creating the dice, practitioners should consider the individual child they will be working with and what specific social skills, connection issues, and emotional regulation challenges that child needs to work on and represent those challenges on the dice. Foam dice come in various sizes and can be found online and in most educational supply stores. The foam dice can be given to the child to take home, and parents and other family members can play this intervention with the child.

Three Foam Dice

Prevention Role-Play

Target Area	Social Skills
Level	Child and Adolescent
Materials	None
Modality	Individual

Introduction

Children and adolescents with ASD and other developmental disorders often find themselves in specific situations or events that create a great deal of anxiety and dysregulation for them. Parents often have a difficult time getting their children to participate in dysregulating events, such as getting their hair cut or going to the dentist. Prevention role-play can help children and adolescents reduce anxiety levels, gain social skills, and desensitize to specific scenarios and events that are typically troublesome for them.

Instructions

Practitioners should begin by identifying what specific situation or event a child is struggling with. More than likely, this can be identified by the parents. For example, the parents identify that going to the doctor is a struggle. The child has had several meltdowns, and often the parents cannot get the child to go into the doctor's office. The practitioner would gather as much information from the parents as possible about going to the doctor, such as the doctor's name, what the office is like, the usual procedures, and the child's specific reaction and behavior. The practitioner then meets with the child and role-plays the situation with the child in a fun, engaging, and somewhat exaggerated way. The practitioner may begin by using puppets or people figures or use him- or herself to play the roles of the child, the doctor, and the parent. The practitioner should use props such as dress-up clothes and masks to make the role-play fun, active, and playful, exaggerating all the reactions. The practitioner will likely use a whole variety of props from the playroom. The practitioner will ask the child to participate in the role-play and let the child participate at the level he or she is comfortable with. The practitioner will encourage the child to take on more and more of the roles until the child is fully participating and playing him- or herself and going through the role-play. When depicting the actual events through role-play has been played several times, the practitioner will introduce playing the role-play with a positive outcome where the child uses coping skills and goes to the doctor without having a meltdown or getting upset. The practitioner and child will then play through the new role-play several times until the end of the session. The role-play may be repeated in the next session and several sessions afterwards until the child can successfully participate in going to the doctor. It is most helpful to begin this intervention a few sessions prior to the event the child will be participating in.

Rationale

Prevention Role-Play is designed to help children practice positive social skills to help them participate in challenging situations or events that create a great deal of anxiety or dysregulation for the child. This intervention also helps children become desensitized to the troubling situation or event. The role-play should be played many times to help the child desensitize to the troubling event.

Practitioners should especially implement this intervention a couple of sessions prior to the child participating in the troubling situation that will be role-played. The practitioner will want to gain feedback from the parents on how the child handled the situation after participating in the prevention role-play intervention. Parents can also role-play with their child at home. Parents will especially want to implement this intervention a few days prior to attending the targeted event.

Prevention Role-Play Problem Situations

Going to the doctor

Going to the dentist

Getting a haircut

Going to a grocery or department store

Going through a car wash

Attending school assemblies

Participating in school field trips

Going to fairs and carnivals

Going to jump houses and arcades

Attending a family reunion

Attending a birthday party

Having relatives visit

Going on a vacation

Flying in an airplane

Going through airport security

Using a public restroom

Ordering food at a restaurant

Going to a theme park

Playing at a park

Going to a swimming pool

Quiet Loud

Target Area	Social Skills
Level	Child and Adolescent
Materials	None
Modality	Individual

Introduction

Children and adolescents with ASD often struggle with their tone of voice. Some children with ASD may present with a flat tone of voice 100 percent of the time while other children with ASD may speak at inappropriate volumes (too quiet or too loud for the situation). The Quiet Loud intervention works on helping children with ASD and other developmental disorders understand tone of voice by recognizing how their voice can fluctuate and how they can control the tone and fluctuation.

Instructions

The practitioner tells the child that they are going to complete an activity that works on how the child speaks and how his or her voice can be quite, loud, or in between. The practitioner demonstrates for the child by pressing his or her hands together in front of him or her and begins by saying something in a whisper. The practitioner moves his or her hands apart slowly and progressively keeps moving his and her hands further apart. While the practitioner is continually moving his or her hands further apart, the practitioner is increasing the loudness of his or her voice. The practitioner then asks the child to do the activity with the practitioner. The child can pick a word to say and that is the word they will use to go from a quiet to loud voice.

The practitioner can follow up the activity with discussing places and situations where it would be appropriate to be quite, talk in a whisper, normal voice, or loudly. The practitioner and child can also practice changing the tone in the child's voice to represent being sad, excited, scared, or any other state by tone of voice.

Rationale

This intervention works on increasing social skills, especially related to speaking in an appropriate volume for the situation and how to fluctuate tone of voice to mirror various feelings and states that the child may be experiencing. It is likely that this intervention will need to be played multiple times to help the child gain mastery and increase their speaking and tone skills. Parents can be taught to practice this intervention at home with their child.

Quiet Loud

School Rules

Target Area	Social Skills
Level	Child and Adolescent
Materials	Paper, Markers, Highlighters
Modality	Individual, Group

Introduction

Children and adolescents with ASD and other developmental disorders often struggle with social skills and social interaction. Arguably, the school setting is the largest social setting that the child participates in and is often the most anxiety producing due to the myriad of social demands. School Rules help the child identify various social situations and rules that the child may encounter and how to better understand social situations and practice developing appropriate skills to navigate the situations that child is struggling with.

Instructions

The practitioner explains to the child that they will be working on improving social skills to help the child follow rules and participate better in school. The child draws a picture of his or her school on a piece of paper. The child writes the rules of his or her school in the picture he or she has drawn. (The rules can be whatever the child can remember about rules to follow at school.) The child then draws an outline of a person beside the school. Inside the outline person, the child writes any social rules that he or she can think of that exist at school. The practitioner may have to explain to the child what is meant by social rules. After the child has completed the drawings and written the rules, he or she goes through each of the rules and colors a dot next to each rule using the following guide:

Green = Rules that he or she does not understand
Pink = Rules that he or she does not like
Yellow = Rules that he or she breaks
Blue = Rules that he or she likes

The practitioner then processes through the rules with the child and specifically addresses the rules that the child does not understand and does not like. The practitioner should also discuss ways to help the child follow the rules that he or she is breaking.

Rationale

This intervention works on increasing social skills to help the child or adolescent navigate school rules and social rules that the child may be struggling with. Parents can be taught this intervention, and a copy of what the child created can be sent home so parents can continue to practice improving the school-related social skill deficits.

School Rules Examples

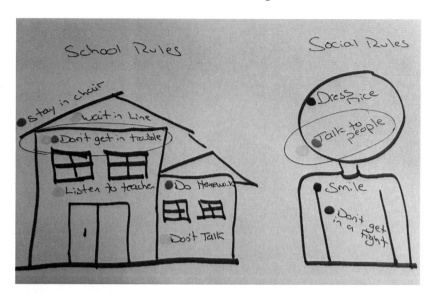

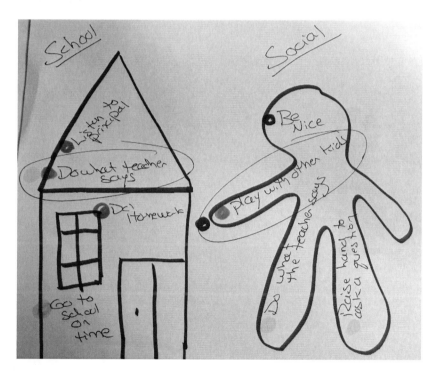

Connection

Touch **Eye Contact** Attuning

Nurturing Caring Eye Gaze

Affection **Attachment** Expression

Love Closeness Joining

Bonding *Relationship* Connection

Reciprocity Tenderness **Care**

Emotion Warmth

Obstacle Course

Target Area	Connection (Relationship Development)
Level	Child and Adolescent
Materials	Several Pieces of Paper
Modality	Individual, Family, Group

Introduction

Children and adolescents with ASD and other developmental disorders often struggle in meaningful connection with others. This intervention helps children work on connection, trust, being present with another person, and general relationship development.

Instructions

The practitioner explains to the child that they will be playing a game to work on trusting and becoming more comfortable with other people. The practitioner wads up several pieces of paper and places them around the playroom. The practitioner then explains to the child that they are going to take turns leading each other from one side of the playroom to the other without stepping on any of the pieces of paper and that the person being led will be wearing a blindfold. The practitioner goes first and blindfolds the child. The practitioner stands behind the child with his or her hands on the child's shoulders. The practitioner guides the child with words and physical prompts across the playroom having the child avoid stepping on any of the pieces of paper. Once successfully across the playroom, the practitioner and child switch roles, and the child leads the practitioner back across the playroom avoiding all the pieces of paper. The game can be played multiple times with the papers being rearranged each time. The practitioner should regularly check in with child to make sure he or she is feeling comfortable with being blindfolded and being physically led by another person.

Rationale

This technique helps children and adolescents work on connection and relationship development. Children and adolescents can work on becoming more comfortable with engaging other people and work on reducing any anxiety that might accompany interacting with others. The practitioner and child can play the intervention several times. Each time they play, they can mix up the pieces of paper on the floor so there is a new obstacle field to guide through. Parents can be taught this intervention to implement at home and encouraged to play regularly with their child and include the entire family. This intervention, along with several of the connection interventions, requires a level of physical touch. This should always be explained to the child before implementation, and the practitioner should confirm with the child that he or she is OK with the level of touch and close proximity of the practitioner.

Obstacle Course

Break Out

Target Area	Connection (Relationship Development)
Level	Child and Adolescent
Materials	Toilet Paper or Crepe Paper
Modality	Individual, Family, Group

Introduction

The Break Out intervention helps children and adolescents attune to another person, recognize their own physical self, and become comfortable with the physical presence of others. Further, it promotes a sensory-based experience that children with ASD typically respond positively to.

Instructions

The practitioner explains to the child that the practitioner is going to wrap the child's legs and arms in crepe paper (toilet paper can also be used), and the child is going to bust out of the wrapping. The practitioner begins by wrapping one part of the child's body such as the child's legs in toilet paper or crepe paper. The child is instructed to remain still until the practitioner has finished wrapping the child's legs. Once the practitioner has finished, the practitioner says, "Go," and the child breaks out of the wrapping. The practitioner then wraps another part of the child's body such as his or her arms and repeats the process. The practitioner can also wrap the child's hands and the child's entire body. If the child wants, the practitioner and child can switch roles, and the child can wrap the practitioner.

Rationale

Break Out helps children and adolescents work on connection and relationship development. It also works on attuning to another person and body control issues. This intervention can be repeated several times. When wrapping the child, the practitioner should wrap the child several times around but not too much. It is important that the child be able to break out of the wrapping easily.

This intervention should be taught to parents to do at home with their child. Parents should be encouraged to make the intervention fun and animated and switch roles with the child, letting the child wrap the parent. Parents can even include the entire family in the intervention.

Break Out

Iguana Walk

Target Area	Connection (Relationship Development)
Level	Child
Materials	None
Modality	Individual

Introduction

Iguana Walk is a simple yet effective intervention that helps children develop relationship and connection with others. It is presented in a fun and playful manner that engages children to participate. Further, it helps children understand and become comfortable with positive touch and closely interacting with another person.

Instructions

The practitioner tells the child that the practitioner is going to do an iguana walk up and down the child's arms and legs. The practitioner should demonstrate on a stuffed animal or the practitioner's own arm first to show the child what will be happening. The child sits on the floor or a chair and holds out one arm. The practitioner makes his or her hands into the formation of talking puppet hands, and one hand at a time, the practitioner clamps onto the child's hand (starting with the child's fingers) and moves up the child's arms clamping onto the child as an iguana might clamp on and walk up the child's arm. The practitioner then repeats the same action for the child's other arm and then the child's legs.

   The practitioner can then ask the child if he or she wants to do the Iguana Walk on the practitioner. The practitioner should be cautious to explain to the child that there will be touch involved and gain permission from the child for each level of touch. The practitioner and child can play the Iguana Walk back and forth several times.

Rationale

This technique helps children work on connection and relationship development especially in attuning to others, becoming comfortable with physical touch, and participating in a reciprocal activity with another person. This intervention can be repeated several times. The practitioner should encourage the child to complete the Iguana Walk on the practitioner, but if the child is not comfortable with this, it should not be forced. This intervention should be taught to parents to do regularly at home with their child. This connection intervention can be paired with other connection interventions for parents to do with their child at home and involve the entire family.

Iguana Walk

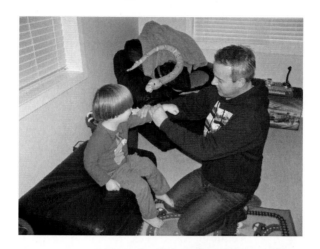

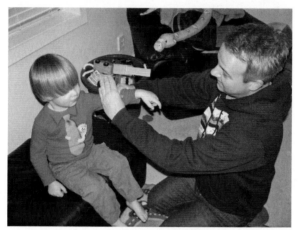

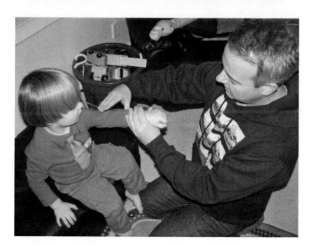

Feeling Card Find It

Target Area	Connection (Relationship Development)
Level	Child
Materials	Index Cards, Pencil
Modality	Individual, Family

Introduction

Children with ASD and other developmental disorders often struggle in connecting with others, even their own family members. Connection skills often include both social skill and emotional regulation components. This intervention helps children develop relationship connection, social skills, and emotional regulation. The practitioner can design this intervention to address specific feelings that the child needs help expressing and regulating.

Instructions

The practitioner and child write feeling words on several index cards (usually 8–10 to begin with). The practitioner and child then take turns picking an index card and hiding it somewhere on their body while the other person is not watching. The other person then has to find the card on the person's body by physically searching for it. When the card is found, the person who found it has to read the feeling word on the card and talk about something that makes him or her feel that emotion. This process is repeated until all the index cards have been completed. The practitioner should hide the cards in fairly obvious places on his or her body. If the child is uncomfortable with being touched or touching the practitioner, then feeling words can be used, and each person can point at different areas on the body.

Rationale

This technique helps children work on social skills, connection and relationship development, and emotional regulation. This intervention can be repeated several times with the practitioner and child creating different index feeling cards. The placement of index cards on the body should be somewhat obvious such as coming out of a sleeve, on top of head, coming out of shoe, etc. This intervention helps children learn to notice and attune to another person, recognize and express emotions, and develop connection. The practitioner can also change the feeling share time to another instruction such as "Make the feeling on your face." This intervention should be taught to parents to do at home with their child. Parents are encouraged to attune to what their child may be feeling and represent those feelings in the index feeling cards. Parents are also encouraged to involve the entire family.

Feeling Card Find It

Ring around Me

Target Area	Connection (Relationship Development)
Level	Child
Materials	None
Modality	Individual

Introduction

Ring around Me is a fun and engaging connection intervention especially for young children. Physical contact is maintained throughout the activity, and social skills such as eye contact are also practiced in this intervention.

Instructions

The practitioner explains to the child that they will be playing a game that requires them to hold hands the entire time. The practitioner stands in one spot, and the child stands beside the practitioner. The practitioner takes the child's right hand, and the child starts to walk around the practitioner. As the child gets to the back of the practitioner, the practitioner switches to his or her left hand and takes the child's right hand as the child continues around the practitioner. The child keeps walking around the practitioner with the practitioner switching hands but always keeping contact with the child as he or she walks around the practitioner.

After several times of walking around, the practitioner can have the child switch directions and walk around the practitioner the opposite direction. The practitioner can also have the child walk around him or her in a specific style such as in slow motion, fast, hopping, skipping, or walking backward.

Rationale

The Ring around Me intervention helps children work on connection and relationship development, especially in attuning to another person, making physical connection, and following another person's instructions. This intervention can be repeated several times, and the practitioner and child can switch roles if the child desires.

This intervention should be taught to parents to do regularly at home with their child. This intervention can be easily paired with other connection interventions for parent and child to play together at home. Parents can also involve siblings or other family members. Involving other family members to play with the child will likely help generalize relationship connection skills.

Ring around Me

Sand Games

Target Area	Connection (Relationship Development)
Level	Child and Adolescent
Materials	Sand Tray, Sand, Various Sand Toys
Modality	Individual

Introduction

Children and adolescents with ASD and other developmental disorders often need help in learning how to connect with others. Further, they often respond well to sensory-based instruction and experiences. Sand Games are sensory-based activities that help develop relationship connection.

Instructions

The practitioner explains to the child that they are going to be doing some activities in a sand tray. The practitioner and child proceed in playing several sand games together.

1. The practitioner and child take turns burying each other's hands and arms in the sand.
2. The practitioner and child create a hand sand sifter, pouring sand from the practitioner's hand to the child's hand back to the practitioner's hand.
3. One person makes a hand cup and the other person fills it with sand.
4. The practitioner and child each bury one hand in the sand and move their hand under the sand trying to grab the other person's hand.
5. The practitioner and child hold hands and place their held hands on top of the sand. With their free hands, the practitioner and child work together to bury the held hands in the sand.

Rationale

The Sand Games intervention helps children work on connection and relationship development. Children can work on becoming more comfortable interacting with another person and working with another person to complete a task. This intervention can be repeated several times, and the practitioner or child can create new sand games to play. Sand Games should actively involve both the child and practitioner doing something together and/or utilizing the other person's hands/arms, etc. This intervention can be taught to parents to do at home with their child if the family has a sand tray. If not, the intervention will be done only in the practitioner's office.

Sand Games

Turn around and Make a Face

Target Area	Connection (Relationship Development)
Level	Child and Adolescent
Materials	None
Modality	Individual, Family, Group

Introduction

Children and adolescents with ASD can struggle in basic interactions with another person such as simply looking at another person. This intervention helps children and adolescents work on noticing and connecting with another person. Further, it works on helping children develop social skills such as looking at others and participating in a joint activity with another person.

Instructions

The practitioner tells the child they are going to play a game where they will be looking at each other. The practitioner and child stand with their backs to each other; on the practitioner's count of 3, the practitioner and child both turn around and make a face at each other. Each person has to say what kind of face the other person was making.

This activity is repeated several times, each time the practitioner and child have to make a different face at each other. The practitioner can also instruct that specific faces have to be made each time, such as turn around and make a silly face, angry face, happy face, confused face, scared face, mean face, friendly face, etc.

Rationale

This technique helps children and adolescents work on connection and relationship development as well as social skills and emotional regulation. With specific instructions from the practitioner, the child can practice making various faces that are displaying emotions and practice making faces that display social awareness such as a friendly face or mean face.

Turn Around and Make a Face helps the child not only work connection but also increases emotional expression and helps the child learn to recognize body language. This intervention should be taught to parents to do regularly at home with their child. The practitioner should give parents several ideas of faces to make and practice when completing this intervention with their child at home.

Turn Around and Make a Face

Fishy and Shark

Target Area	Connection (Relationship Development)
Level	Child
Materials	None
Modality	Individual

Introduction

Playing with another person, paying attention to others, and engaging in physical contact with another person are typical struggle areas for children with ASD and developmental disorders. This intervention helps children work on developing these skills in a playful and engaging process.

Instructions

Fishy and Shark is a hand game that is done between the practitioner and the child. The practitioner and child sit on the floor across from each other but close enough to touch. The child could also sit on a chair with the practitioner on the floor. The practitioner puts his or her hands together and moves them across the floor wiggling them like a fish swimming. The practitioner wiggles his or her hands toward the child saying, "Fishy, fishy." When the practitioner gets close to the child, the child says, "Shark," and takes his or her hands and clamps down on the practitioner's hands that are making the fish. This intervention should be repeated several times, and if the child desires, the roles can be switched, and the child can be the fishy and the practitioner can be the shark.

Rationale

Fishy and Shark helps children work on connection and relationship development, especially in attuning to and paying attention to another person. This intervention also incorporates increasing concentration, eye contact, and joint attention skills.

Fishy and Shark should be taught to parents, and parents should be encouraged to play this intervention with their children regularly at home. This intervention can be included with other connection interventions so parents can play several connection interventions during one play time. Parents can also try to incorporate other family members to play this intervention with the child.

Fishy and Shark

Magnify Me

Target Area	Connection (Relationship Development)
Level	Child
Materials	Magnifying Glass
Modality	Individual

Introduction

Magnify Me is a fun and engaging way for children to work on relationship connection. This intervention helps children interact positively with others, notice others, be comfortable being noticed by others, and develop a better sense of the child's physical self.

Instructions

The practitioner explains to the child that the practitioner will be using a magnifying glass to closely examine different parts of the child. The practitioner uses a toy magnifying glass and looks through the glass moving over different parts of the child, such as the child's ear, nose, eyes, hair, fingers etc. As the practitioner moves over a part of the child, he or she should make positive comments such as "Wow, you have such a cool nose!" or "This is some really brown hair."

It is important that the practitioner make comments about the child and that the comments be positive and/or descriptive. The practitioner should then try to get the child to switch roles and have the child look through the magnifying glass at the practitioner. This intervention can be played several times with the practitioner making new comments as he or she examines the child.

Rationale

This technique helps children work on connection and relationship development. Magnify Me helps children become more comfortable and aware of their own self and more comfortable with and aware of others. Further, the magnifying glass creates a fun component that also provides a safe distance for the child as he or she works on these skills. This intervention can be taught to parents to play at home and can be combined with other connection techniques that parents can play with their children regularly between counseling sessions.

Magnify Me

Crawling Crabs

Target Area	Connection (Relationship Development)
Level	Child
Materials	None
Modality	Individual

Introduction

Children with ASD often need to work on various connection skills in a way that is less anxiety producing and more playful and engaging. Crawling Crabs is a simple yet effective connection and touch intervention that helps children (especially young children) develop relationship with others. Further, it helps children understand and become comfortable with positive touch, attuning to another person, and engaging in a mutual process with another person.

Instructions

The child sits on the floor with his or her legs stretched forward and his or her hands on his or her legs. The practitioner sits across from the child and starts moving his or her hands with fingers down on the floor in a walking movement toward the child. When the practitioner reaches the child, the practitioner continues with his or her hands walking up the child's legs and then up the child's arms until the practitioner reaches the top of the child's arms. At the top of the child's arms, the practitioner gently squeezes the child's shoulders.

The practitioner should explain the game to the child before beginning and complete a demonstration of the movement on a stuffed animal or on the practitioner's own legs and hands. Crawling Crabs should be repeated several times. The practitioner and child can also switch roles if the child desires.

Rationale

Crawling Crabs helps children work on connection and relationship development as well as concentration and eye contact. This intervention should be taught to parents to do regularly at home with their child. Parents may also combine this intervention with other connection interventions and try to incorporate other family members to play with the child.

As with any touch intervention, practitioners and parents should try to be aware of and understand the child's limits in terms of being comfortable with or having a sensory sensitivity to physical touch. Before beginning any intervention that involves touch, practitioners should reference the Association of Play Therapy's "Paper on Touch" available at www.a4pt.org.

Crawling Crabs

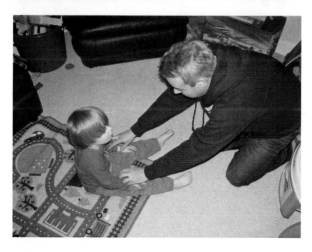

Silly Glasses

Target Area	Connection (Relationship Development)
Level	Child and Adolescent
Materials	Several Eye/Sunglasses, Mirror
Modality	Individual, Family, Group

Introduction

Silly Glasses is a fun technique to help children notice and pay attention to themselves and others. There is an interactive component for a child that promotes participating and connecting with others. Joint attention skills are also developed in this intervention.

Instructions

The practitioner explains to the child that they will be playing a game using several different glasses. The practitioner displays several different eyeglasses or sunglasses for the child to choose from. The more sunglasses and the more variety of sunglasses that are available will keep the intervention going and make the intervention more interesting to the child.

The practitioner explains to the child that they are going to take turns picking out a pair of sunglasses and putting the sunglasses on the other person. (It is important that each person chooses the sunglasses and places the sunglasses on the other person; the sunglasses should not simply be handed to the other person.) Once the sunglasses are in place, the practitioner and child look in a mirror to see themselves in their sunglasses. This process is repeated several times with the practitioner and child going through several sunglasses.

Rationale

This technique helps children work on connection and relationship development, especially in regard to noticing another person and reciprocally interacting with another person. Children also work on improving eye contact with this intervention. Practitioners are encouraged to assemble several different styles and types of eyeglasses, sunglasses, and silly play glasses.

This intervention should be taught to parents to do regularly at home with their child. Parents should try to incorporate other family members to play this intervention with the child. Parents will need to collect and have available several types of glasses. Some suggested options for collecting sunglasses would be yard sales and flea markets where the cost would typically be less.

Silly Glasses

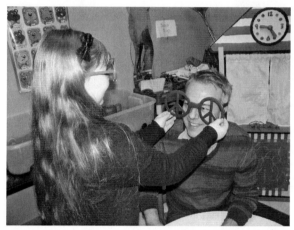

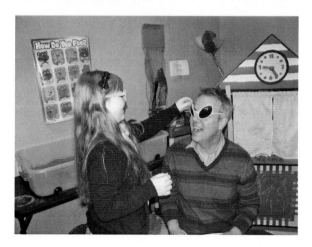

Hands, Hands, Hands

Target Area	Connection (Relationship Development)
Level	Child and Adolescent
Materials	Piece of Paper, Pencil
Modality	Individual, Family, Group

Introduction

Children and adolescents with ASD often feel uncomfortable or are unsure with physical touch. This intervention provides a simple and fun way to engage a child with ASD with a variety of physical touch activities that are presented in play form. The practitioner can engage the child in one, two, or several hand activities. The intervention can easily be modified to fit the child's comfort level.

Instructions

The practitioner explains to the child that they are going to play several games connecting with their hands. The practitioner instructs the child to trace around his or her hand on a piece of paper. The practitioner then instructs the child to write on the traced hand all the positive things he or she can think of to do with his or her hands that involves another person.

Once the child is finished, the practitioner can add to the list if the practitioner can think of other positive things. (Several ideas are included here.) The practitioner and child then do or pretend to do all the things on the list. The practitioner also discusses with the child how connecting with others can be positive and can feel good.

Rationale

This technique helps children and adolescents work on connection and relationship development. Children learn several positive ways (that are playful and feel good to the child) that he or she can connect with others through physical touch games. During the intervention, the practitioner should discuss with the child how interacting with others can feel good and be a positive experience and that playing with other children can be enjoyable.

This intervention can be taught to parents to do regularly at home with their child. Parents may need help in coming up with several positive things to do with hands so the practitioner should provide a list of examples for the parents.

Hands, Hands, Hands

Example Activities

Thumb wrestling

High five

Pat on the back

Hand massage

Head massage

Ear massage

Shoulder massage

Patty cake

Holding hands

Creating a special hand shake

Hand stack game

Intertwining fingers

Lotion hands

Pretend palm reading

Drawing on person's
    back with your finger

Tickling

Arm wrestle

Painting fingernails

Washing hands

Hug

Palm press

Interlocking fingers

Dancing

Finger face painting

Finger press

Hand slap (grab) game

Fist pump

Handshake

Pinky swear

Ring around the Rosy game

London Bridge game

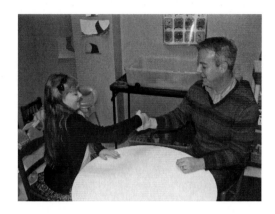

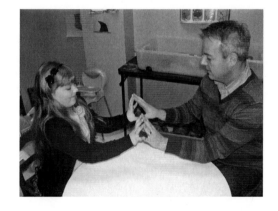

Sculpture

Target Area	Connection (Relationship Development)
Level	Child and Adolescent
Materials	None
Modality	Individual, Family, Group

Introduction

Sculpture connects the child and practitioner together in a way that the child has to pay attention to and notice the practitioner. It also incorporates a physical component that helps with connection between child and practitioner. Children are able to work on becoming more comfortable with physical touch and interacting with others while engaging in a playful activity.

Instructions

The practitioner instructs the child that they are going to take turns making each other into sculptures. The practitioner goes first and moves the child into whatever position he or she needs the child to be in for making the child into a sculpture of something. The practitioner should physically move the child into position by touching the child's arms, legs, etc. and moving them into position, not simply using verbal commands. Once the child has been made into a sculpture, the child has to guess what he or she has been made into.

The practitioner and child then switch roles, and the child gets to make the practitioner into a sculpture of something. This intervention can be repeated several times with the practitioner and child making each other into several different sculptures.

Rationale

This technique helps children and adolescents work on connection and relationship development, especially interaction with another person and participating in physical touch. The intervention should be repeated several times, and the practitioner and child should take turns creating each other into a sculpture. It is important that physical touch be included by having the person creating the sculpture physically move the other person into the positions, not just giving verbal instructions.

The practitioner will want to make sure that the child is comfortable with the level of physical touch involved. The intervention can be taught to parents to do at home regularly with their child, and the entire family can play together.

Sculpture

Aluminum Wrap

Target Area	Connection (Relationship Development)
Level	Child
Materials	Aluminum Foil
Modality	Individual

Introduction

Children with ASD can have challenges with sensory issues when trying to connecting with other people. This intervention works on both sensory processing and being present with and connecting to another person. It also provides a reciprocal component that is beneficial for relationship development.

Instructions

The practitioner explains to the child that they are going to use aluminum foil to wrap different parts of their bodies. The practitioner begins by wrapping one of the child's hands in aluminum foil and pressing in lightly on the aluminum foil so it molds around the child's hand. The practitioner then takes the aluminum foil off the child's hand and wraps the child's other hand. The practitioner can wrap the child's feet, ears, fingers, anything that would be appropriate but only one body part at a time. The practitioner should notice the child's reaction and be sensitive to the child as each body part is wrapped.

The practitioner should ask the child how it feels when one of his or her body parts is wrapped in aluminum foil. The practitioner should try to engage the child in switching roles and having the child wrap the practitioner's hands and feet in aluminum foil. Once the practitioner and child are finished wrapping each other with aluminum foil, the aluminum foil should be used to make something for each other that the other person can wear on themselves, such as a hat or bracelet.

Rationale

This technique helps children work on connection and relationship development. It also works on sensory tactile and touch issues and physical pressure. This intervention can be repeated session to session. It can also be taught to parents to do at home with their child periodically. It is important to have the child switch roles and be in both positions: being wrapped and wrapping. The child may prefer one role over the other, and it may take time to get the child to switch roles.

Aluminum Wrap

Silhouette

Target Area	Connection (Relationship Development)
Level	Child and Adolescent
Materials	White Paper, Pencil
Modality	Individual

Introduction

This intervention provides the opportunity for the practitioner to connect with the child and for the child to pay attention to and reciprocate back to the practitioner and create a visual representation of that connection. Silhouettes can be simplified or made more complex depending on the comfort and functioning level of the child.

Instructions

The practitioner explains to the child that they will be using paper and pencils to trace different body parts. The practitioner has the child lay his or her head down sideways on a white piece of paper. The practitioner traces around the child's head. The child then draws his or her features on the tracing. The child then traces the practitioner's head while the practitioner lays his or her head down on a white piece of paper.

The practitioner and child then trace each other's hands and lastly feet (if appropriate and the practitioner and child are both comfortable with tracing feet). The traced hands and feet can be colored and decorated by the child. If the practitioner has a large enough piece of paper, the child can lie on the paper and have their whole body traced. The practitioner should try to get the child to reciprocate and trace the practitioner. If the child is not willing to do this, the practitioner should just trace the child. For adolescents, the practitioner should talk with them about what parts of their body they are comfortable tracing before the intervention is started.

Rationale

This technique helps children and adolescents work on connection and relationship development. The practitioner should introduce the intervention to the child so the child understands they will be tracing each other's head, hands, and feet on a white piece of paper. The practitioner will want to ensure that both children and adolescents are comfortable with the intervention before beginning. This intervention can be taught to parents to do at home with their child on a regular basis.

Silhouette

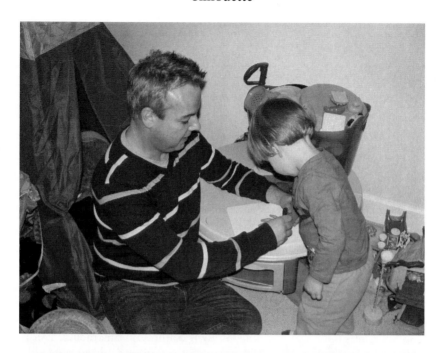

Family Spin

Target Area	Connection (Relationship Development)
Level	Child and Adolescent
Materials	None
Modality	Individual, Family, Group

Introduction

This intervention is typically completed as a family play activity. It can be completed with just the practitioner and child but tends to work better with a family or in a group setting. It provides an opportunity for family members to connect and engage with the identified child or adolescent with ASD in a playful game that works on connection and relationship development.

Instructions

The practitioner instructs the family to make a circle and each family member to put both of their hands in the circle (out in front of them) and everyone grab someone else's hands. Each family member should be holding another family members hand so the whole family is connected. The practitioner then instructs the family that they will start spinning around to the right slowly. After a period of time, the practitioner will interject various instructions for the family to do, such as speed up, walk in slow motion, start spinning to the left, stop, jump, hop to the right, etc. The practitioner can also play this game with a child one on one, and the practitioner and child can take turns being the person who gives the instructions. If the family plays this game at home, one person can be designated as the person who will give the family instructions on how to spin. Each family member can have a turn in this position.

Rationale

This technique helps children and adolescents work on connection and relationship development, especially in making eye contact, attuning to others, and physical touch. This intervention is a family intervention and can be done with one parent and one child or multiple family members. It can also be implemented in a group format. The size does not matter as long as there are at least 2 people. When the family does the intervention at home, it is helpful if there is one person who stays on the outside of the circle calling out the instructions. If there is no one to do this, then the parent should interject the instructions as he or she plays with the child.

Family Spin

Our Unique Greeting

Target Area	Connection (Relationship Development)
Level	Child and Adolescent
Materials	None
Modality	Individual, Family, Group

Introduction

Children and adolescents with ASD and other developmental disorders often have challenges in greeting others. This intervention creates the opportunity for the practitioner to create a unique greeting with the child or adolescent that can involve many elements but should involve some physical touch. This intervention helps improve social skills as well as connection ability.

Instructions

The practitioner explains to the child that they will be creating a unique greeting that they can give each other each time they see each other. Hands, gestures, and words can all be used in creating the greeting. The practitioner and child can use their unique greeting each time the child comes in for a session. The practitioner and child can also create a unique way to say goodbye at the end of each session.

The greeting and goodbye should involve some form of physical touch. The practitioner should allow the child to try and come up with the greeting and goodbye on their own. The practitioner should assist the child as needed. Once the practitioner and child have created their unique greeting and goodbye, the practitioner and child should practice the greeting and goodbye several times.

Rationale

This technique helps children and adolescents work on connection and relationship development in the areas of physical touch, acknowledging and attuning to another person, and creating special meaning in a relationship. Once the special greeting and goodbye have been created and practiced, the practitioner will want to make sure that he or she remembers them so the next time he or she sees the child, the special greeting and goodbye can be implemented.

This intervention can be taught to parents to do at home with their child. Each parent and other family members if appropriate can all create a unique greeting and goodbye rituals with the child. The greeting and goodbye rituals should always contain a physical touch component.

Together Balloons

Target Area	Connection (Relationship Development)
Level	Child and Adolescent
Materials	Balloon
Modality	Individual, Family, Group

Introduction

Children and adolescents with ASD and other developmental disorders often need practice in connecting with others and working with and cooperating with others. Together Balloons provides a fun and engaging way for the practitioner and child to work on connection. This intervention also incorporates social skill development in the areas of working together to complete a task and making eye contact.

Instructions

The practitioner explains to the child that they will be playing a game together that involves a balloon. The practitioner blows up a balloon and explains to the child that they are going to work together in a special way to keep the balloon in the air.

The practitioner and child stand facing each other and grab each other's hands and hold both hands. The practitioner hits the balloon in the air, and the practitioner and child have to keep the balloon from touching the ground. The practitioner and child maintain holding hands the whole time and move around together to keep the balloon in the air. If the balloon hits the ground, it should be picked up and the game started again. The game can be repeated several times.

Rationale

This intervention helps children and adolescents work on connection and relationship development through physical touch, working cooperatively, and attuning to and being aware of others. Together Balloons can be taught to parents to do at home regularly with their child. Other family members can also get involved and play with the child. This intervention works well as a family play activity and a group activity. In a family or group setting, the participants can pair up or function as one large group holding each other's hands.

Together Balloons

Hide and Find

Target Area	Connection (Relationship Development)
Level	Child and Adolescent
Materials	Index Cards, Pencil
Modality	Individual

Introduction

Children and adolescents with ASD and other developmental disorders often have challenges in establishing relationships and meaningful connection with others. This intervention provides several opportunities for the child or adolescent to practice relationship and connection skills. A variety of other skills can be easily incorporated in this intervention such as social skills and emotional regulation improvement.

Instructions

The practitioner tells the child they are going to play a game where the child is going to find some things the practitioner hides in the room. The practitioner writes various connection activities on index cards and hides the index cards around the playroom. (The child should be waiting outside the playroom door or standing in a corner and not watching.) Once the practitioner is finished hiding the cards, the child then enters the playroom and has to find all the index cards.

When the child finds an index card, he or she has to do the activity with the practitioner that is written on the index card. The practitioner should create around 5–7 index cards. Connection activities should be short and simple. Some examples include shaking hands, making eye contact, giving a hug, giving a double high five, giving a pat on the back, thumb wrestling, etc.

Rationale

This technique helps children and adolescents work on connection and relationship development through a variety of methods (some examples are included here). The practitioner can write any connection-related activity on an index card. The practitioner can also include activities that work on improving social skills and emotional regulation. The intervention should be taught to parents to do at home. Parents will likely need to be given several ideas for connection activities that can be written on index cards. Parents will need to prepare several index cards and play the intervention using around 7 cards; they can play the intervention several times, creating a new set of index cards/connection activities each time they play.

Hide and Find

Example Activities

Shake hands

Make eye contact for 10 seconds

Give a hug

Give a double high five

Give a pat on the back

Thumb wrestle

Have a staring contest

Play patty cake

Play the hand stack game

Lotion each other's hands

Draw a picture together

Give a fist pump

Feed each other candy

Hold hands and walk around the room

Give a hand or back massage

Look at each other and make a face

Do a face painting

Do a dance together

Bury each other's hands in the sand

Squiggle Drawing Gift

Target Area	Connection (Relationship Development)
Level	Child and Adolescent
Materials	White Paper, Pencil
Modality	Individual, Family, Group

Introduction

Children and adolescents with ASD do tend to feel connection to important people in their lives but often lack ability to show that connection. This intervention provides the opportunity to work on connection with another person, and it creates a strong visual element to help reinforce learning and remembering the connection. It also presents the opportunity for children to show another person they are thinking about them and acknowledge them in a meaningful way. This intervention is adapted from Donald Winnicott's Squiggle Technique (Berger, 1980).

Instructions

The practitioner explains to the child they will be doing a drawing activity. The practitioner and child each take a piece of white paper and a pencil. When the practitioner says, "Go," they both start squiggling all over the paper. This lasts about 10 seconds, and then the practitioner says, "Stop." The practitioner and child exchange papers, and each one has to make a drawing out of the other person's squiggle to present back to the other person as a gift.

After the practitioner and child have finished their drawing, they share with each other what they created for each other and then give the drawings to each other as a gift. The practitioner and child should both sign each drawing, showing that they completed it together. The practitioner and child can then complete another Squiggle Drawing Gift; there is no limit on the number of times the activity can be played.

Rationale

This technique helps children and adolescents work on connection and relationship development by thinking about and creating something for another person. It also provides the opportunity for the child to create something collaboratively and practice giving another person a gift. The practitioner and child can repeat the squiggle drawing intervention several times. Parents should be taught how to do this intervention at home and instructed to play it with their child regularly. This intervention also works well in a group setting with each participant pairing up and rotating through the group, creating several drawings.

Squiggle Drawing Gift

(Child turned squiggle into a dragon to give to practitioner)

(Child turned squiggle into sailing trip to give to practitioner)

My Measurements

Target Area	Connection (Relationship Development)
Level	Child
Materials	Measuring Tape
Modality	Individual

Introduction

Children with ASD often need to engage in connecting activities to become more comfortable and confident in relationship skills. This intervention is a fun way to promote relationship connection. The practitioner can adjust this intervention to be simple, with 1–2 measurements conducted, or be more complex by conducting several measurements. The adjustment should match the child's functioning level, comfort level, and developmental level.

Instructions

The practitioner explains to the child that the practitioner is going to conduct several measurements of the child. Before beginning, the practitioner should give the child an example, such as "I am going to measure the length of your arm." The practitioner should then demonstrate the measuring on the practitioner's own arm.

The practitioner conducts various measurements on the child and writes down the child's measurements on a piece of paper. The practitioner should try to get the child to engage in a reciprocal process having the child conduct some measurements on the practitioner. Some of the types of measurements can include measuring the child's legs, arms, head, feet, hands, height, ears, smile, nose, hair length, fingers, etc.

Rationale

This intervention helps children work on connection and relationship development especially in the areas of physical touch, receiving positive attention from another person, and engaging in reciprocal and joint attention processes. A cloth or flexible measuring tape works best for this intervention. The practitioner should try to incorporate fun measurements such as the length of the child's smile and the length of the child's fingers. Making the intervention silly and fun will make the intervention more engaging and comfortable for the child. Parents should be taught how to do this intervention at home and encouraged to play the intervention regularly with their child at home. Parents can keep track of the measurements and show the child each time the measurements change.

My Measurements

I Am a Tree, We Are a Family

Target Area	Connection (Relationship Development)
Level	Child
Materials	None
Modality	Family, Group

Introduction

This intervention is implemented in a family or group setting. This intervention promotes connecting with other people and working together to accomplish a task. Both relationship development and social skill development are incorporated in this intervention.

Instructions

The practitioner explains to the family that they will be working together to create a short and fun skit that they will perform for the practitioner. The practitioner should designate a stage area in the room where the skit will be performed. The family has to choose one person who will lead out the skit and be the tree. The tree goes first and moves to the stage area, makes a tree shape, and says, "I am a tree." The family has to decide who will go second, third, and so on. Each person will be something different that naturally connects to a tree. Some examples might be grass, leaves, roots, a bird, a squirrel, a piece of fruit, an acorn, moss, etc. For example, the second person to go might be a leaf: That person would go next and move to the stage area, physically connect (however they choose) to the "tree" person, and say, "I am a leaf." Then the third person would go and so on. Once the last person has gone, then the family says in unison, "We are a family."

The family should be given as much time as they need to create the skit (although it will likely not take long). They will need to decide the order that each person will go in and what each person will be. Once the family has finalized the skit, they will perform the skit in front of the practitioner. If the family would like, they can perform a second skit with each family member choosing different parts to perform.

Rationale

This intervention helps children work on connection and relationship development and social skills, especially in the areas of physical touch, attuning to other people, and working as a group to accomplish a task. The practitioner should give the full instruction to the family before they begin and then allow them time to put together their skit. Once the skit has been performed, the practitioner should applaud and congratulate the family. The practitioner might suggest creating another skit with the identified child as the tree if he or she was not the tree the first time.

Body Bubble Target

Target Area	Connection (Relationship Development)
Level	Child
Materials	Bubbles
Modality	Individual, Family, Group

Introduction

Children with ASD tend to respond positively to bubbles. This intervention uses bubbles in a fun and engaging way that promotes connection and relationship development skills. Body Bubble Target also incorporates social skill development in the areas of noticing others and spatial awareness in regard to personal body space.

Instructions

The practitioner explains to the child that they will be playing a game that involves bubble blowing. The practitioner and child decide who will blow the bubbles first. The other person will stand somewhere in the room and make a circle target with his or her arms and hands. The bubble blower has to stand a certain distance from the target. (The practitioner can decide the appropriate distance.) The bubble blower tries to blow as many bubbles as he or she can through the bubble target that the other person is making with his arms and hands. After he or she has successfully blown several bubbles through the target, the practitioner and child can switch roles.

The practitioner and child can keep switching roles and playing the intervention throughout the whole session. Whoever is the target, can change the target position to vary the game. Some examples might be making a circle in front of the person, making a circle above the head, making a circle beside the body, making the circle larger or smaller, etc.

Rationale

This intervention helps children work on connection and relationship development, especially in the area of attuning to another person. This intervention also works on spatial and body awareness and joint attention skills. Parents can be taught how to implement this intervention at home and can be encouraged to play with their child and involve other family members.

Body Bubble Target

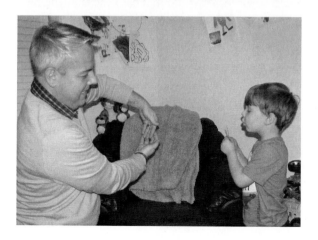

Bubble Tag

Target Area	Connection (Relationship Development)
Level	Child
Materials	Bubbles
Modality	Individual, Family, Group

Introduction

Bubble Tag incorporates two fun and engaging games for children—bubble blowing and tag. Connection and relationship development skills as well as social peer play skills are addressed in this intervention. Bubble tag works well as in individual intervention but can also be played in a family or group setting.

Instructions

The practitioner explains to the child that they are going to play a game of tag using bubbles. The practitioner and child decide who will blow bubbles first. That person will blow bubbles and try to tag (hit) the other person with a bubble. The other person should move around the room and try to avoid getting hit by any bubbles. Once the person is hit by a bubble, the two switch roles. The game moves back and forth with each person tying to tag the other person with bubbles until the practitioner ends the game. The game can be lengthened by requiring a person to be tagged by a certain number of bubbles; for example, decide that 10 bubbles have to hit he person before the two switch roles.

This intervention should be played in a playroom or other room setting where the space is somewhat restricted. It should not be played outside. Playing outside or in a large space would make it very challenging for the bubble blower to ever catch someone with the bubbles.

Rationale

This intervention helps children work on connection and relationship development skills as well as social peer and group play. The child may prefer to stay in one role such as the bubble blower, but the practitioner should encourage the child to switch roles as each role addresses different skill areas. Parents can be taught to implement this intervention at home and can be encouraged to play with their child. The whole family can participate and play with one bubble blower or assign multiple family members as bubble blowers working together to tag the rest of the family.

Bubble Tag

Flower, Rain, and Sun

Target Area	Connection (Relationship Development)
Level	Child
Materials	None
Modality	Individual

Introduction

Children with ASD often have challenges in attuning to and playing with another person. This intervention promotes connection and relationship development as well as joint attention and play skills with another person. Flower, Rain, and Sun also promotes increasing comfort with physical touch and sensory processing. It is a quick, easy, and fun intervention to implement with children.

Instructions

The practitioner explains to the child that they will be playing a game that involves some physical touch. The practitioner may want to complete a demonstration on a stuffed animal before implementing the intervention with the child so the child is prepared for what will be happening. The practitioner begins by making a fist and telling the child that the fist is a flower that wants to grow. The flower needs sun and needs to be watered. The child should pretend to give the flower water and sun. The practitioner then slowly opens his or her fist and spreads his or her fingers out representing the flower blooming. The practitioner tells the child that he or she can smell the flower, touch or feel the flower, or pretend to pick a petal from the flower. The practitioner then pretends to be a snapping flower and when the child touches or smells the flower, the practitioner will gently close up his or her hand on the child's finger or nose.

The practitioner and child can play the intervention several times growing several new flowers. The practitioner and child can also switch roles, and the child can pretend to make a flower. The practitioner will want to make sure that he or she explains the game to the child before they begin so the child is not startled by the practitioner implementing the snapping flower component. If the child is uncomfortable with this element, it can be left out of the intervention.

Rationale

This intervention helps children work on connection and relationship development, especially in regard to attuning to another person, participating in a reciprocal activity, and being comfortable with physical proximity and touch. Parents can be taught to play this intervention with their child. This intervention can be implemented with several other connection interventions, as most connection interventions will not require much time to complete.

Flower, Rain, and Sun

Hello Friend

Target Area	Connection (Relationship Development)
Level	Child
Materials	None
Modality	Family, Group

Introduction

This intervention is implemented in a family or group setting. Hello Friend is a variation of the "Namaste" greeting in yoga for children with autism and special needs. This intervention promotes connection and relationship development as well as making eye contact, following instructions, and participating in a group. This intervention is adapted from Louise Goldberg's *Creative Relaxation* (Goldberg, 2013).

Instructions

The practitioner explains to the family or group that they will be implementing a special greeting to each other that will be done in a unique format. The family or group will form 2 circles, an inside circle and an outside circle. The outside circle will be facing the people in the inside circle, and conversely the inside circle will be facing the people in the outside circle. Each person will begin by holding the hands of the person in front of them, so a person in the inside circle will reach forward and hold hands with a person in the outside circle.

Once everyone is holding someone else's hands, each person will great the other by saying "Hello friend" 3 times to the tune of "Three Blind Mice." Once Hello Friend has been said 3 times, the outside circle shifts to the right, and now each person is facing a new person. They again hold hands and say, "Hello friend" 3 times to the tune of "Three Blind Mice." This continues until the outside circle has shifted back to their original people.

Rationale

This intervention helps children work on connection and relationship development as well as social skills, especially in the areas of physical touch, attuning to other people, working as a group to accomplish a task, greeting another person, and group peer play skills. This intervention works best with a larger number of people, typically recommended for a family or group with at least 5 members. Practitioners can learn more about Louise Goldberg's work at www.yogaforspecialneeds.com.

Appendix
Additional Resources

Author's Note: This chapter contains various assessment materials, forms, and other useful worksheets that can be downloaded in a larger, printable format from www.autplaytherapy.com/resources.

Feelings List

Accepted	Afraid	Affectionate	Loyal
Angry	Miserable	Anxious	Misunderstood
Peaceful	Beautiful	Playful	Ashamed
Brave	Awkward	Calm	Proud
Capable	Quiet	Bored	Overwhelmed
Caring	Relaxed	Confused	Cheerful
Relieved	Defeated	Comfortable	Safe
Competent	Satisfied	Concerned	Mad
Depressed	Pressured	Confident	Provoked
Content	Desperate	Regretful	Courageous
Silly	Lonely	Rejected	Curious
Special	Disappointed	Remorseful	Strong
Discouraged	Disgusted	Sad	Sympathetic
Excited	Embarrassed	Shy	Forgiving
Thankful	Sorry	Friendly	Thrilled
Fearful	Stubborn	Nervous	Stupid
Glad	Understood	Frustrated	Good
Unique	Furious	Tired	Grateful
Valuable	Guilty	Touchy	Great
Hateful	Happy	Helpless	Hopeful
Wonderful	Hopeless	Humorous	Worthwhile
Unattractive	Joyful	Uncertain	Lovable
Humiliated	Uncomfortable	Loved	Hurt
Ignored	Impatient	Indecisive	Inferior
Insecure	Irritated	Jealous	Worried

Social Skills Checklist

NAME_____DATE_____

☐ Listening	☐ Asking Questions
☐ Starting a Conversation	☐ Smiling
☐ Ending a Conversation	☐ Saying "Thank You"
☐ Introducing Self	☐ Making Eye Contact
☐ Introducing Other People	☐ Basic Boundaries
☐ Asking for Help	☐ Following Instructions
☐ Apologizing	☐ Asking Permission
☐ Sharing	☐ Joining in a Group
☐ Helping Others	☐ Taking Turns
☐ Appropriate Body Language	☐ Appropriate Tone of Voice
☐ Understanding Personal Space	☐ Two-Way Conversation
☐ Making and Maintaining Friends	☐ Public Boundaries
☐ Handling Losing	☐ Handling Winning
☐ Giving Instructions	☐ Convincing Others
☐ Negotiating	☐ Using Self-Control
☐ Handling Bullying	☐ Giving Compliments
☐ Accepting Consequences	☐ Managing Disagreements
☐ Recognizing Trouble Situations	☐ Understanding Humor
☐ Completing Tasks without Assistance	☐ Initiating Tasks
☐ Well-Rounded Play Skills	☐ Problem Solving
☐ Flexibility	☐ Advanced Boundaries
☐ Expressing Emotions Appropriately	☐ Knowing Emotions
☐ Recognizing Emotions in Others	☐ Expressing Affection
☐ Expressing Concern for Others	☐ Handling Anxiety
☐ Emotion/Situation Appropriateness	☐ Showing Compassion
☐ Handling Anger-Related Feelings	☐ Avoiding Fights
☐ Dealing with Accusation	☐ Standing Up for Others
☐ Self-Relaxation Techniques	☐ Accepting "No"
☐ Other_____	

Toys and Materials List

Functional Toys
Kitchen • Food • Dishes • Baby Dolls • Doll House • Miniature People • Miniature Animals • Cars, Trucks, Boats • Bowling Set • Basketball Goal • Cash Register • Doctor's Kit • Tool Kit Blocks • Toy Phone • Toy Camera

Expressive Materials
Paper • Markers and Crayons • Paints • Play Doh Clay • Dry Erase Board and Markers • Stickers • Beads • Ribbon • Pipe Cleaners • Confetti • Pom Poms • Puppets • Dress Up Clothes and Hats • Mr. Potato Head • LEGOs

Sensory Toys
Sand Tray • Water Tray • Moon Sand • Kinetic Sand Rice or Bean Tray • Snow Mobility • Sensory Balls • Theraputty • Tangle Toys • Sidewalk Chalk • Fidget Toys • Musical Instruments • Slinky • Whirly Wheel • Koosh Ball • Magnets

Brain-Based Toys
Punching Bag • Hula Hoops • Bean Bags • Brain Puzzles • Balloons • Bubbles • Ring Toss • Rubik's Cube • Origami Kit • Mini Trampoline • Word Search • Word Scramble • Seek and Find Games

Board Games
Find It • Bop It • Jenga • Chairs • Pick-Up Sticks • Jacks • Barrel of Monkeys • Animal Logic • Blokus • Rush Hour • Twister • Spot It • Stare I Spy • Story Cubes • Memory • Chicky Boom • Hed Banz

Play-Based Intervention-Tracking Sheet

Play-Based Intervention	Target Area Addressed (Emotional, Social, Connection)	Date Administered	Child/Adolescent Response

Create-Your-Own-Technique Worksheet

Name of Technique: _____

Area(s) Addressed (circle all that apply): Emotional Regulation, Social Skills, Connection Other: _____

Level (circle one): Child, Adolescent, Both

Modality (circle all that apply): Individual, Family, Group

Materials Needed:

_____

_____

_____

_____

Practitioners should be able to answer the following questions with a "yes" response:

Is the technique directive?

Is the technique concrete and not a metaphor?

Does the technique address real situations/issues that the child is struggling with?

Does the technique refer back to the child's treatment goals?

Can the technique be adjusted from simple to more complex?

Does the technique take into account different developmental levels?

Is the technique low prop based?

Can the practitioner participate with and assist the child if needed?

Is the technique simple to explain and complete (not too many steps)?

Can the technique be taught to parents to implement at home?

Description of Technique:

_____

_____

_____

_____

_____

_____

_____

_____

_____

_____

_____

_____

Goals of Technique:

_____

_____

_____

_____

_____

_____

_____

Additional Information:

_____

_____

_____

_____

Apps for Autism and Developmental Disabilities

Meebie

This app assists children and adolescents in identifying emotions and various degrees of expression using the Meebie doll and several accessory pieces. Meebie provides a strong, engaging visual element to help with emotional regulation ability.

Touch and Say by Interbots

This app helps children learn various skills, such as colors, numbers, and letters, but also has an eye contact and feelings component. There is also a talk component where the app will mimic what the child says. This app is visually appealing and interactive.

Face-Cards

This app presents several different feelings that can be chosen, and an accompanying face is displayed showing the emotion. There is also an iGaze video that helps work on making and maintaining eye contact. The emotions faces are all female and provide good expressions.

Emotions Flash Cards for Kidz

This app presents several emotions categorized into three categories: positive, neutral, and negative. When a feeling is selected, a flash card showing an animated face displaying the emotion appears. This app offers a thorough index of emotion flash cards.

Autism Aide: Teach Emotions

This app focuses on the emotions of happy, sad, hurt, ashamed, anger, bored, and scared. When a feeling is chosen, several different animated faces showing the emotions are displayed. There is an option to record someone saying the emotion word and an option to select background music.

Emotions (Teaching Tool for Speech and Language Development)

This app has five categories for helping with emotional regulation: 1) identifying pictures with emotions, 2) identifying emotions with a picture, 3) identifying picture-based scenarios with an emotion, 4) identifying pictures with labels based on scenarios, and 5) identifying pictures based on scenarios. Children are given options to choose from, and the pictures are of real people displaying emotions. This app is full of strong visuals and multiple ways to learn emotional regulation.

ABA Flash Cards

This app goes through several flash cards displaying real people showing emotions. When each flash card is presented, there is an auditory voice saying what the feeling is. The pictures are very good, and there are several feelings presented.

FeelingOmeter

This app uses a temperature gauge design to represent and help children learn about various feelings and levels of feelings. Children can choose from several feelings and choose colors to go with their feelings. Pictures can also be used to help display feelings. This app provides several elements that all combine together well to help children increase their emotional regulation ability.

Self-Regulation Training Board by Brad Chapin

This app helps children identify warning signs that correspond with a certain feeling, the feeling itself, and a strategy that the child can do when he or she is feeling the emotion. This app has a strong visual and seems appealing and engaging.

Zones of Regulation

This app is a thoroughly developed app that has several levels (reminiscent of popular video game design) and helps children learn about and develop emotional regulation ability. There are several components, and each one has strong visual elements and engaging levels for the child.

Stories2Learn

This app focuses on creating social stories. Several predesigned stories are available for viewing. The predesigned stories can be edited, and there is the option for creating your own social stories. This app is well designed and easy to use for making and viewing social stories.

Language Lab Spin & Speak

This app displays a board game that works on social skills. Up to 5 players can play at one time. This app addresses several social skills and is visually engaging and fun.

Choiceworks

This app includes working on emotional regulation, a waiting timer display, and a visual schedule. The components are all well represented and easy to follow with auditory prompts. There is a short accompanying book with each component.

FindMe

This app is designed to help children improve their social and attention/concentration skills. Several scenes are presented that become increasing more challenging in identifying the target person in the picture while several distractions are happening.

Kimochis Feeling Frenzy

This is a fun, playful, and engaging app that helps children distinguish between positive and negative emotions and helps children identify various emotions. There are four different levels so children can begin on an easy level and progress to more challenging levels.

iTouchiLearn Feelings

This app presents several options for helping children learn about and identify emotions. There is a feelings section where children can watch a feeling being performed and identify what feeling is being displayed. There is a games section with various interactive games that work on feeling identification, and there is a music section that presents feelings through music.

Puppet Pals

This app presents several stages (scenes) to choose from and several different characters to choose from to create your own puppet show. Children can record the story using their own voice and then watch the story back. Practitioners can also record stories made specifically for children and have the children watch the stories. There is also a Puppet Pals II.

Story Maker

This app allows children to create their own stories with audio and pictures. Several pictures are provided, and personal pictures can be used. This app is easy to use with lots of options. Practitioners can also create stories designed specifically for the children they work with.

CBT4Kids

This app was developed by two clinical psychologists and provides a fun, engaging, and informative approach based on cognitive behavioral therapy. Practitioners can enter in actual children and track their progress. There are several interactive tools such as a relaxation and breathing game.

Time Timer

This is a simple but effective app. A timer is displayed that represents 1 hour. Users can select how much time they want put on the timer, and the time counts down with a red visual. This is a very useful app for parents and practitioners who want to use a strong visual aid to help children stay on task and understand amounts of time.

ZoLo

This app presents various shapes and sounds that children can manipulate to create fun and whimsical designs and play sculptures. There is a strong creative and sensory component that is very engaging.

Internet Resources

Play-Based Treatments

AutPlay Therapy, www.autplaytherapy.com
Autism Movement Therapy, www.autismmovementtherapy.com
The Theraplay Institute, www.theraplay.org
Filial Therapy, www.play-therapy.com
RePlays, www.drkarenlevine.com
Floortime, www.stanleygreenspan.com
The Play Project, www.playproject.org
Creative Relaxation, www.yogaforspecialneeds.com
Social Stories, www.thegraycenter.org
Do 2 Learn, www.do2learn.com
Model Me Kids, www.modelmekids.com
The Social Express, www.thesocialexpress.com
Liana Lowenstein, www.lianalowenstein.com

Toys/Games/Supplies

The Self Esteem Shop, www.selfesteemshop.com
Child's Work Child's Play, www.childswork.com
Child Therapy Toys, www.childtherapytoys.com
Play Therapy Supply, www.playtherapysupply.com
Therapy Shoppe, www.therapyshoppe.com
Therapro, www.therapro.com
Fun and Function, www.funandfunction.com
Fat Brain Toys, www.fatbraintoys.com

Organizations and Resources

One Place for Special Needs, www.oneplaceforspecialneeds.com
The Missouri Autism Report, www.moautismreport.com
Children with Special Needs, www.childrenwithspecialneeds.com
Autism Society of America, www.autism-society.org
National Autism Association, www.nationalautismassociation.org
HollyRod Foundation, www.hollyrod.org
Association for Science in Autism Treatment, www.asatonline.org
Families for Early Autism Treatment, www.feat.org
Autism Consortium, www.autismconsortium.org
CHADD, www.chadd.org
ADDitude, www.additudemag.com
National Fragile X Foundation, www.fragilex.org
FRAXA, www.fraxa.org
National Tourette Syndrome Association, www.tsa-usa.org
National Down Syndrome Society, www.ndss.org

Down Syndrome Research Foundation, www.dsrf.org
Apraxia-KIDS, www.apraxia-kids.org
NADD, www.thenadd.org
American Assoc. on Intellectual and Developmental Disabilities, www.aaidd.org
The ARC, www.thearc.org
Association for Play Therapy, www.a4pt.org
Play Therapy International, www.playtherapy.org
British Association of Play Therapists, www.bapt.info

References and Suggested Readings

American Psychological Association. (2013). *Diagnostic and statistical manual of mental disorders* (5th ed.). Washington, DC: Author.

Association for Play Therapy. (2015). *Paper on Touch*. Available: www.a4pt.org

Attwood, T. (2006a). *Asperger's and girls*. Arlington: Future Horizons.

Attwood, T. (2006b). *Asperger's syndrome*. Philadelphia: Jessica Kingsley Publishers.

Attwood, T. (2007). *The complete guide to Asperger's syndrome*. Philadelphia: Jessica Kingsley Publishers.

Bass, J. D., & Mulick, J. A. (2007). Social play skill enhancement of children with autism using peers and siblings as practitioners. *Psychology in the Schools*, 44(7), 727–735.

Berger, L. R. (1980). The Winnicott Squiggle Game: A vehicle for communicating with the school-aged child. *Pediatrics*, 66(6), 921–924.

Booth, P. B., & Jernberg, A. M. (2010). *Theraplay*. San Francisco, CA: Jossey-Bass.

Brady, L. J., Gonzalez, A. X., Zawadzki, M., & Presley, C. (2011). *Speak, move, play and learn with children on the autism spectrum*. Philadelphia, PA: Jessica Kingsley Publishers.

Bratton, S. C., Ray, D., Rhine, T., & Jones, L. (2005). The efficacy of play therapy with children: A meta-analytic review of treatment outcomes. *Professional Psychology: Research and Practice*, 36, 376–390.

Cavett, A. M. (2010). *Structures play-based interventions for engaging children and adolescents in therapy*. West Conshohocken, PA: Infinity Publishing.

Centers for Disease Control. (2014). *Autism spectrum disorders*. Atlanta, GA: Author.

Coplan, J. (2010). *Making sense of autistic spectrum disorders*. New York: Bantam Books.

Cross, A. (2010). *Come and play: Sensory integration strategies for children with play challenges*. St. Paul, MN: Redleaf Press.

Dawson, G., McPartland, J., & Ozonoff, S. (2002). *A parent's guide to Asperger's syndrome and high functioning autism*. New York: The Guilford Press.

Delaney, T. (2009). *101 games and activities for children with autism, Asperger's, and sensory processing disorders*. New York: McGraw Hill.

Dienstmann, R. (2008). *Games for motor learning*. Champaign, IL: Human Kinetics.

Drewes, A. A. (2009). *Blending play therapy with cognitive behavioral therapy*. New Jersey: John Wiley and Johns Inc.

Exkorn, K. S. (2005). *The autism sourcebook*. New York: HarperCollins Publishers.

Gallo-Lopez, L., & Rubin, L. C. (2012). *Play based interventions for children and adolescents with autism spectrum disorders*. New York: Routledge.

Gil, E. (1994). *Play in family therapy*. New York: The Guilford Press.

Goldberg, L. (2013). *Yoga therapy for children with autism and special needs*. New York: W. W. Norton & Company.

Grandin, T. (2006). *Thinking in pictures*. New York: Random House.

Grant, R. J. (2012). *Parent-led social skills groups*. Springfield: Robert Jason Grant Ed.D Publishing.

Grant, R. J. (2016). *AutPlay therapy handbook*. Springfield: Robert Jason Grant Ed.D Publishing.

Greenspan, S., & Wieder, S. (2006). *Engaging autism*. Cambridge, MA: Da Capo Press.

Griffin, S., & Sandler, D. (2010). *Motivate to communicate*. Philadelphia, PA: Jessica Kingsley Publishers.

Hull, K. B. (2011). *Play therapy and Asperger's syndrome*. Lanham, MD: Jason Aronson.

Jernberg, A. M., & Booth, P. B. (2001). *Theraplay: Helping parents and children build better relationships through attachment-based play*. New Jersey: John Wiley and Sons Inc.

Josefi, O., & Ryan, Y. (2004). Non-directive play therapy for young children with autism: A case study. *Clinical Child Psychology and Psychiatry, 9*, 533–551.

Kenny-Noziska, S. (2008). *Techniques, techniques, techniques: Play based activities for children, adolescents, and families*. West Conshohocken, PA: Infinity Publishing.

Knell, S. M. (1997). *Cognitive behavioral play therapy*. Lanham, MD: Rowman and Littlefield.

Kuypers, L. (2011). *The zones of regulation*. San Jose: Think Social Publishing.

Landreth, G. L. (1991). *Play therapy: The art of the relationship*. Muncie, IN: Accelerated Development Inc. Publishers.

Laushey, K., & Heflin, L. J. (2000). Enhancing social skills of kindergarten children with autism through the training of multiple peers as tutors. *Journal of Autism and Developmental Disorders, 30*(3), 183–193.

Levine, K., & Chedd, N. (2007). *Replays*. Philadelphia: Jessica Kingsley Publishers.

Lindaman, S., & Booth, P. B. (2010). Theraplay for children with autism spectrum disorders. In P. B. Booth and A. M. Jernberg (Eds.), *Theraplay: Helping parents and children build better relationships through attachment-based play* (3rd ed., pp. 301–358). San Francisco: Jossey-Bass.

Lowenstein, L. (1999). *Creative interventions for troubled children and youth*. Toronto, ON: Champion Press.

Lowenstein, L. (2002). *More creative interventions for troubled children and youth*. Toronto, ON: Champion Press.

Lowenstein, L. (Ed.). (2008). *Assessment and treatment activities for children, adolescents, and families: Practitioners share their most effective techniques*. Toronto, ON: Champion Press.

Lowenstein, L. (Ed.). (2010). *Assessment and treatment activities for children, adolescents, and Families. Volume 2: Practitioners share their most effective techniques*. Toronto, ON: Champion Press.

McIntyre, T. (2014). *Behavior Advisor*. Available: www.behavioradvisor.com

Moor, J. (2008). *Playing, laughing and learning with children on the autism spectrum*. Philadelphia, PA: Jessica Kingsley Publishers.

Notbohm, E., & Zysk, V. (2004). *1001 great ideas for teaching and raising children with autism spectrum disorders*. Arlington, TX: Future Horizons.

Parker, N., & O'Brien, P. (2011). Play therapy reaching the child with autism. *International Journal of Special Education, 26*, 80–87.

Phillips, N., & Beavan, L. (2010). *Teaching play to children with autism.* Thousand Oaks: Sage Publications.

Ray, D. (2011). *Advanced play therapy: Essential conditions, knowledge, and skills for child practice.* New York: Routledge.

Rogers, S. J., & Dawson, G. (2010). *Early Start Denver Model for young children with autism.* New York: The Guilford Press.

Ross, R. H., & Roberts-Pacchione, B. (2007). *Wanna play.* Thousand Oaks, CA: Corwin Press.

Schaefer, C. E. (2003). *Foundations of play therapy.* New Jersey: John Wiley and Sons Inc.

Schaefer, C. E., & Kaduson, H. G. (2010). *101 favorite play therapy techniques volume II.* Lanham, MD: Jason Aronson.

Sherratt, D., & Peter, M. (2002). *Developing play and drama in children with autistic spectrum disorders.* London: Fulton.

Sicile-Kira, C. (2004). *Autism spectrum disorders.* New York: The Berkley Publishing Group.

Sicile-Kira, C. (2006). *Adolescents on the autism spectrum.* New York: The Berkley Publishing Group.

Sohn, A., & Grayson, C. (2005). *Parenting your Asperger child.* New York: Penguin Group.

Stillman, W. (2005). *The everything parents guide to children with Asperger's syndrome.* Avon: Adams Media.

Stillman, W. (2007). *The autism answer book.* Naperville: Sourcebooks, Inc.

Thornton, K., & Cox, E. (2005). Play and the reduction of challenging behavior in children with ASD's and learning disabilities. *Good Autism Practice*, 6(2), 75–80.

VanFleet, R. (2013). *Filial therapy: Strengthening parent-child relationships through play.* Sarasota: Professional Resource Press.

Index